CHEATING
IN A NUTSHELL

WHAT INFIDELITY DOES TO THE VICTIM

WAYNE & TAMARA MITCHELL

First published September 2019

Interior and Cover Design: Istvan Szabo, Ifj/Fiverr
Cover Photo: Marie C. Fields/Shutterstock

ISBN 978-1-948158-03-9 (hardcover)
ISBN 978-1-948158-00-8 (paperback)
ISBN 978-1-948158-02-2 (kindle)
ISBN 978-1-948158-01-5 (epub)

Published by Third Ghost Press

WayneAndTamara.com

"Men's courses will foreshadow certain ends, to which, if persevered in, they must end. But if the courses be departed from, the ends will change."

—Charles Dickens, A Christmas Carol

TAMARA'S ACKNOWLEDGEMENT

Thanks to Lynda Buffat, as best friend and first reader, for substantial contributions to the manuscript.

WAYNE'S ACKNOWLEDGEMENT

Two regular readers of our *Direct Answers* advice column were especially helpful. Thanks to Sandra Stout, first reader of the finished manuscript, for her constant encouragement and helpful suggestions. Thanks to Susan Voskuil for allowing us to see into a reader's mind and pointing out how the book applies to other aspects of life.

CONTENTS

PREFACE

We never planned on writing an advice column. Twenty years ago, the creative director of one of the largest U.S. newspaper syndicates saw something we wrote and asked us to submit sample columns. Creating those columns lit a flame. It became the first step in a service project that continues to this day.

After a month passed without hearing anything from the syndicate, we distributed the column ourselves. An hour and a half after sending out a few emails, we had our first newspaper. Six weeks later, we were in five or six papers in the U.S. and Canada. Two years later, the column was in newspapers in twelve countries.

Before long we were straining to answer all the letters we received. The letters came from musicians and chefs, ranchers and housewives, business people, factory workers, and a minister performing weddings, even as he doubted his own marriage would last. Some letters were full of misspellings; others ended with an imposing title and a corporate address.

Over the years, one group of letters stood out, not simply because there were so many of them but because the writers' wounds were fresh even when their injury had been inflicted years before. These were the letters from those betrayed by the person they were dating, living with, engaged to or married to.

The letters followed a predictable course. Though our feelings often surprise us, our emotions follow universal patterns. Betrayal feels like betrayal for a reason, and there are reasons it is so hard to forget.

In *Cheating in a Nutshell*, we retell stories we were told. None of the stories is exceptional; each is typical of the experience. Many times we balance a story with contemporary research, but our book doesn't depend on that research. Fads and perspectives in social science change, but the experience of being betrayed does not.

We wished we could have answered all the letters we received because we knew how much pain the writers were in. Of the many letters we answered, we wish we could have answered at greater length, but there wasn't time. If we had found a book on infidelity we could recommend, we would have recommended it. But there was no such book, so we knew in time we would write this book.

This book is the longer answer we wanted to give each person who wrote us. Before writing the book, we reread over 3,000 cheating letters from the first 10 years of our column. As we wrote we had three groups of people in mind:

Those just learning their partner has deceived them.

Those who stayed with a cheating partner and now realize things cannot be restored.

Those betrayed in a past relationship, who seek a deeper understanding of what happened.

We hope this book will encourage the next generation of researchers—perhaps now only undergraduates—to take infidelity research in a more accurate and factually correct direction.

In *Cheating in a Nutshell*, we discuss emotional infidelity alongside physical infidelity rather than treating it as a separate topic. We do this because the two share much in common and because emotional infidelity is often only the cover story for deep physical involvement. The damage from each is similar. Beyond that, emotional involvement is at the center of all our relationships. Admitting to emotional involvement may make the betrayal even worse.

Last, let us say, if we have a point of view, it is because the facts point in one direction. We cannot find a way to make the case for a different point of view. In *The House on the Strand*, a novel by Daphne du Maurier, the main character is a man named Dick Young. At one point Dick says, "Truth is the hardest thing to put across."[1] We agree, and we would define truth as that which corresponds to facts. Truth is not what we wish to be true or what we would hope to be true. Truth is what corresponds to facts.

Thousands of people wrote us. They had a story to tell. This book is the explanation of that story.

CHAPTER 1
YOUR WORLD OVERTURNED

"There are times when fortune inflicts wounds that simply won't heal, when the story of a life breaks into two distinct sections, a before and an after."

—Maurizio Viroli, biographer

My wife attended night classes with a former workmate and friend. He is really good-looking and so is she. On the last night of class together, I followed them to a bar. After they came out, she gave him a big hug.

They drove down a dark road and parked in a poorly lit small park. I couldn't see what they were doing, but I can only imagine. Forty-five minutes later, they drove back to where she was parked and hugged. I couldn't tell if they kissed.

When my wife got home, she was very nervous. Later, when we were in bed, I asked her if she went out and celebrated. She said no. I asked why she and her friends didn't go to a bar or do something. She said they got out late.

When I asked if our friend was there, she said he had to leave early. Every time I gave her a chance to tell me what she did, she lied and not only lied but sounded sure about it. After a couple of hours of not being able to sleep, I woke her up. She again denied doing anything.

After a long silence, I told her I knew she was at the bar. She said, "Yes, I forgot, I had one drink and came right home." Finally, I told her I knew everything. She would not confess to being in the park until I told her I saw them together. Then she said all they did was talk.

5

I called our friend the next day and asked him the same questions. He lied. When I told him what I knew, he could hardly talk. My wife said she would call our friend and tell him not to call her anymore. He wasn't supposed to know I was listening, but it sounded like they talked beforehand and got their story straight.

Before this she hardly ever wanted sex, and I had to ask. Now she is all over me. She won't show me her phone records from work or her work cell phone. She says they would be hard to get, but she is the facility coordinator, so she can get just about anything.

I love my wife but only want the truth. We can work through this if only she will be honest. I guess my question would be if you think they had something going on.

-Frank

The pattern of the betrayal is familiar, even archetypal: admit nothing. If that is not possible, admit only what is already known. It is the same pattern played out in police stations and criminal courts every day. As one woman told us about her cheating husband, "Denial has become his best friend." There is simply no advantage to a cheater in telling the truth, nor will there ever be. The advantage lies in denial and minimizing. That's what Frank, the author of this letter, learned the hard way.

Usually affairs are discussed as if they are a single act of betrayal. They are not. Even a one-night stand consists of scores of mental acts, and an ongoing relationship with a third party represents thousands of separate mental acts of deception. In the letter above, Frank's wife decided to:

- Meet another man in a bar
- Leave with the other man, instead of going home
- Get in the other man's car, not her own
- Drive to a secluded location
- Engage in acts she would conceal from her husband

At each one of these points, and many others, she could have stopped. But she didn't. When confronted by her husband, she chose to lie repeatedly. Frank came into the last thirty minutes of a two-hour movie. He wants to know the plot, and he has only one person to ask. He is thinking in terms of staying with his wife and saving his marriage. He thinks in those terms because he was not doing anything to end the marriage.

His wife approaches the situation from a different direction. She was looking at another relationship, and possibly her next marriage. Why does she lie? First, out of self-defense. She doesn't want to be found out, and she doesn't want to be told that she is doing wrong. Second, she has justified to herself the *why* behind what she is doing. She gave herself permission in advance, and her objective is to conceal the reason.

She won't give Frank her phone records. Even if she can, it is not to her advantage. In her mind his truth does not exist, her justifications do. The longer she holds him off, the muddier the details become, and the more power that stays in her hands. Frank is in the strongest position to act the night he finds out, but he has the least information and the least ability to do so.

He will never know the whole story, except by inference, but inference is a powerful way of knowing when we know how to use it.

When Michigan anthropologist Laura Betzig did a study of 160 different societies, she found that marriage is as close to a universal human behavior as anything you can name.[1] Looking at this broad cross section of humanity, she isolated 43 different causes of divorce and found that, across cultures, the single most frequently reported cause of divorce is adultery.

In Matthew's gospel he remarks, if Mary had been unfaithful, Joseph would have divorced her. Matthew, who wrote the most complete account of the Sermon on the Mount, reports that Jesus of Nazareth offered adultery as the one clear case where divorce is permitted. "But I tell you that anyone who divorces his wife except for adultery..."[2]

Why do so many religions and legal systems make allowances for adultery as an instance where divorce is allowed? Why is there such a strong taboo against infidelity? There must be a reason deep within us, and that reason must link to our loathing for turncoats, traitors, and embezzlers. It must link to our fears of abandonment.

On our desk now are three letters. The first one is from a young woman who works for an international health organization. She says she married the first man she had sex with. He is the only man she truly loved, but now he stays out all night and won't say where he has been. They have two children. The couple often argue and their daughter misses school with headaches and a nervous stomach.

She hates what her husband is doing, and her family tells her to leave him. "What will happen to the kids?" she wonders. "Will they be broken and maladjusted? The idea of divorce is a big step and the consequences paralyze me."

The second letter is also from a woman, a young journalist married for eight years. Her husband hired an 18-year-old girl to help her with household chores then he started an affair with her. That infidelity ended, but two months before the journalist delivered a baby girl, her husband started a relationship with another woman, 23.

When she confronted that woman, she learned her husband told her that his wife was mentally unstable and promiscuous. That was the lure he used to give the other woman permission to cheat with him. The letter writer sums up her feelings simply. "I have begun to hate the very idea of marriage."

In the third letter, a wife discovers text messages from another woman on her husband's phone. When she asks who the woman is, her husband simply answers, "Why?" So the wife called the number herself. The woman answering claimed she hadn't seen her husband in months. Later, it turned out she saw him that very morning. "I hate him for doing this to our marriage and to my love," the wife told us. "I feel like something inside me died, and I don't know how to recover."

The reaction of these women is universal. Their letters could have come from any part of the world, and, in fact, they did. The first woman lives in Nairobi, the second in Mumbai, and the third in Texas.

A study by psychologist Israel Charny and S. Parnass asked therapists to describe an extramarital affair they were familiar with.[3] The affair might involve a client, a friend, a relative, or the therapists themselves. Of the 62 cases reported, the results were:

- 34% ended in divorce because of infidelity
- 43.5% continued but were rated distressed or unhappy
- 6% were rated blah or empty
- 9% were rated improved

Why do affairs have such impact on the betrayed person?

In his book *Twenty Ads That Shook the World*, James Twitchell tells the story of a company with a marketing problem.[4] This company wanted to sell colorless rocks with almost no practical value. About all you can do with them is use them for drill bits, but that is a tiny market. Not only that, the darn things last indefinitely. Even worse, they are in tremendous over-supply. They are found in abundance in South Africa, Zaire, Ghana, Namibia, Botswana, Australia, Siberia, and many other places.

That was the problem handed to the advertising firm N. W. Ayer & Son. Their client, De Beers Consolidated Mines, had made some inroads with consumers after World War I by linking the giving of diamonds to engagement and marriage. But selling this product was a challenge, and the Ayer copywriters were stumped.

Then, one day in April 1947, one of their copywriters, Frances Gerety, put her head down in exhaustion. How, oh how, could she link romance, essentially valueless stones, and human needs in a way that would sell these rocks? In an inspired moment she wrote the famous phrase De Beers would trademark: "A Diamond is Forever."

It was a brilliant solution. A diamond is forever. Your love is forever. Their love for you is unique. It is also forever. That is what a diamond has come to symbolize, and that feeling is what cheating undermines.

No one has to teach a 16-year-old girl to feel jealous when another girl gives her boyfriend attention. No one has to teach the 16-year-old boy to feel sick to his stomach or angry enough to fight when an older boy moves in on his girl. These feelings are not learned. They are innate. In the depth of our consciousness we want the one for us. That is what we crave.

In 2001, the National Marriage Project hired the Gallup organization to survey a statistically representative sample of never-married adults in their twenties.[5] The results showed 94% agreed with "when you marry you want your spouse to be your soul mate, first and foremost." Eighty-eight percent of single men and women agreed "there is a special person, a soul mate, waiting for you somewhere out there." And nearly every one of those singles thought they would find that person.

In 2007, a survey of Millennials done by Georgetown University found virtually identical results.[6] While the results among women may not be surprising, what accounts for the results among young men? The only adequate explanation is that it is in us to want "the one." Furthermore, studies done on newlyweds report that nearly all of them expect their marriage to last a lifetime.[7] This is true even when they have been informed of the high rate of divorce.

In the Christian Bible, four horsemen are said to be heralds of a last judgment. Infidelity has its own four horsemen. They are disgust, anger, suspicion, and trauma. These four horsemen trample the victim of cheating, and they are more than mere heralds. Each is a judgment on the state of a relationship. Each changes who you are. Like nuclear waste, each has a long half-life. In this book each will get its own chapter.

If you have been cheated on for the first time, you face a situation you have never encountered. Thrust into an emotionally new position, you flounder. This is not your venue, not your forte. In *Cheating in a Nutshell*, we intend to give you a foundation of knowledge. We want to give you a way of thinking about what happened and a way to find the best outcome based on your circumstances.

To help you, we will start the next chapter with a story and a question.

CHAPTER 2
DISGUST

*"You grow more and more a stranger to me at each word.
And I had loved you so..."*

—C. S. Lewis, author

I met a man last year when I was traveling. Everybody inside the aircraft knew he was after me because he asked the person next to me to swap seats with him. I had no clue who he was until someone told me he's a somebody, a wealthy and respected divorced businessman. I, on the other hand, am a struggling businesswoman trying to plant my roots in Africa.

That's when it started. He would call, and I would fly and see him. In short, I became like part of the furniture in any meeting room he was in. Most of the top people in his company know me and my role in his life. He introduces me to prominent people without a hint of embarrassment.

I asked myself a million times if he is for real. The answer is always yes. I can see he's so proud of me and adores me. He also invited me numerous times to his place in Africa, where 90 percent of his investments are located, but I couldn't find the time.

When one of my projects required me to be away three months, he fell tired of phoning. I presumed he was gone but remained faithful and single though temptations are all over the place and the queue is long. When my business plans didn't work out, I emailed him, thanking him for his friendship and telling him I was relocating to start afresh.

He begged and begged me to come to his place and help him in some areas of his business that he cannot monitor. I accepted. I stay in his house, have my own room, and am treated like a queen. I was trying to figure out my place in his life when I noticed something wasn't right. Almost every morning I heard the sound of shoe heels in the corridor. There was no doubt the heels belonged to the lady who looks after his house.

I am not a jealous or suspicious person, so I tried to ignore it, but one day, in the middle of a conversation, I inquired. He said he could not answer. I was shocked. I wanted to grab my bags and run to the airport and catch any flight. He tried to explain his difficult situation, the work he is doing, and the needs of a divorced person. I listened, but in the back of my head I was disgusted. I felt like throwing up.

-Margarite

Before you read further, take a moment and ask yourself a question. Why did Margarite feel like vomiting? That may sound like an odd question, or maybe an obvious one, but the answer to that question is the subject of this chapter.

Ask most people to name the emotions and they will mention love, anger, fear, sadness, and maybe a few others. One thing they are unlikely to mention is disgust, yet contemporary researchers consider disgust one of the primary human emotions.

San Francisco psychologist Paul Ekman has spent his life studying facial expression, emotion, and deception. Ekman began his career thinking we learn facial expressions from those around us and from our culture. That was the common view at the time, but Ekman knew Charles Darwin thought differently.[1] Darwin believed facial expressions are universal; in other words, people who are angry, afraid, or sad make the same face no matter what part of the world they come from.

Ekman sought to test that idea by showing pictures of faces to people in countries as diverse as Japan, Argentina, the United States, and Papua New Guinea.[2] What he discovered is that human beings have seven unique

14

facial expressions which express seven different emotions. These emotions are sadness, disgust, anger, surprise, fear, happiness, and contempt, and people around the world can identify the emotion expressed by a face.

That finding is supported by something which has been known for a long time. People blind since birth show the same facial expressions as those who are sighted.[3] In addition, drivers involved in a near accident display the fear face whether they are alone or with a passenger.[4] That indicates we don't show an expression for someone else's benefit; rather, we feel the emotion and it spreads over our face.

Other researchers have studied the emotions in different ways. Some look at the nervous system,[5] some look at behavior,[6] and still others simply ask people about their feelings.[7] One group of investigators started with dictionaries. They jotted down all the words describing feelings found in the dictionaries of various languages. Then they grouped the words into a few common categories. In that way they hoped to isolate the universal human emotions.[8] But whatever method researchers choose they seem to agree that disgust is a genuine, powerful human emotion.

Ekman and many others have concluded that because expressions of emotion are not socially learned, they developed over the long course of our history on the planet. To take a simple illustration, we all experience fear, but we are not inherently afraid of a downed power line.[9] That is something we must be taught. But let a power line drop in a snake-like coil and we flinch or withdraw when we see it. This suggests that evolution has had enough time to create in us an automatic response to snakes but not to electrical wires.

Our feelings are triggered by things important for our survival and for the survival of our distant ancestors. We have our emotions for a reason, and the reason isn't trivial. Ekman compares emotions to the operating instructions of a computer program, and he says if we try to interfere with these instructions, we are in for a Herculean struggle "precisely because we can't delete or rewrite them."[10]

When one man emailed us about his wife, suspecting she had an affair, he reported, "I can't sleep at night, and every time I think about it my stomach churns. I want to throw up. I can't sleep and I can't work either. I don't know if I can take it."

A woman tells us, "I am the mother of two young children and struggling to survive emotionally. When I was three months pregnant with my second child, and on Cloud Nine, I came home to catch my husband having an affair. I was stunned. The worst part of it all was that all three of us worked in the same office. My husband left the office. However, I returned to work after maternity leave and had to deal with seeing her on a regular basis. Needless to say, I had a few 'come aparts.' The other woman has a reputation of going after married men, but that still doesn't make me feel better. Every time I hear her name or see her, it makes me sick to my stomach, and the wound opens up again. I don't feel as if I will ever feel happy again."

This stomach-churning emotion is disgust. In the body we feel it as nausea, and in the mind we perceive it as revulsion. People describe their physical reaction to discovering an affair with words like nausea, vomit, upchuck, puke, and throw up. They describe their feelings in images of loathing and repugnance.

Disgust makes us distance ourselves from what triggered it. It makes the body queasy and revolts the mind. But its function is not negative; it is positive. Disgust is a guardian. It is the emotion designed to protect us from contamination. Psychologist Paul Rozin, and his colleagues Jon Haidt and Clark McCauley, theorize that disgust began as a physical reaction that protects the mouth from swallowing what is harmful.[11] Originally it had a limited function to protect us from eating rotten food or plants that previously made us sick. That's one reason most people cannot eat a food that gave them food poisoning. It now disgusts them.

Disgust makes us avoid foul smells and things that taste bad, but it doesn't stop there. Rozin and his colleagues suggest that, in time, disgust expanded from protecting our body to protecting us from things which are sickening in a general sense, like unsavory people and unsavory situations. That is why we find turncoats and sleazy politicians unpalatable. We can't trust them. They make us sick to our stomach. They are morally repugnant. Rozin, Haidt, and McCauley summarized the history of disgust by saying, "A mechanism for avoiding harm to the body became a mechanism for avoiding harm to the soul."[12]

Perhaps the most thoughtful writer on disgust is not any psychologist but the lawyer William Ian (Bill) Miller. Miller, a professor of law at the University of Michigan, wrote *The Anatomy of Disgust,* an entire book on the subject.[13] Miller sees disgust in a broader sense as something that includes cringing and recoil.[14] He doesn't believe disgust originated in the mouth; he thinks it originated with touch and smell.[15] Miller's logic is simple. We needed something to warn us before we put a toxic or foul substance in our mouth.

In Bill Miller's mind, disgust marks the boundaries of the self.[16] Our bodies and our minds are set apart from others, and physical intimacy and touching are privileged activities. Forced intimacy is unacceptable. It constitutes a social breach, and, if severe, a crime. We don't share our hopes and dreams, our thoughts and doubts, our failings and our concerns with just anyone. They are available only to those we have invited into our lives. Our public self may be available to everyone who sees us, but our private self is available by permission only.

Love, however, opens the boundaries of the self. It gives permission to come closer. As Miller says, the first light touch on another's arm in effect asks a basic question. "Do I disgust you?"[17] Boundaries are put aside for the one we love, but when that person violates our trust, disgust boots them from our inner circle. Some people say love and hate are opposites, while others claim the opposite of love is indifference. But Miller suggests the true opposites are love and disgust, because we cannot love what disgusts us.[18]

There is a reason we have disgust not as a thought but as an emotion, a bodily reaction. It marks danger. It seizes our attention and won't let go unless we do what it demands. A woman told us about her boyfriend. Five months into their relationship, she discovered pages from the personals in his apartment with some ads circled. There was also a script of what he would say when he called the women. "When I found those ads," she wrote, "I felt sick to my stomach."

Yet she is still with him. Though they broke up twice, he promised and begged and pleaded his way back into her life. They are now on their third couples therapist,[19] and even more tellingly, she was once a relationship therapist herself. As she says, "I'm therapeutically trained. I have read almost every self-help book there is." But the point she won't accept is that disgust once aroused is nearly impossible to eradicate. As psychologist Paul Rozin said, quoting a Nebraska garage mechanic, "A teaspoon of sewage would spoil a barrel of wine, but a teaspoon of wine would do nothing at all for a barrel of sewage."[20]

Disgust repeats itself over and over in letters we receive about cheating. A young woman finds notes her boyfriend has been writing to another woman. "When I read them, I literally got sick to my stomach. I puked. They were disgusting." Another woman returns to her boyfriend's apartment the day after going by herself to an out-of-town concert. On the kitchen calendar, in his ex-girlfriend's handwriting, she sees two freshly written words: "Don't Ask." She tells us, "I was mortified to think of what happened in our apartment in our own bed. I literally threw up. I can't take it."

We began this chapter by asking why Margarite, the businesswoman in Africa, felt like throwing up. The answer is, when the man she cared about admitted to sexual intimacy with his housekeeper, it disgusted her. It disgusted her in the same way it disgusted a young Marine officer who wrote us. The previous year, his wife, his girlfriend at the time, cheated with another Marine who lived in an apartment he passed every day. "I married her even after I found out because I love her and because I feel that everyone deserves a second chance."

The other apartment is now empty and the other Marine stationed on the opposite coast, but this man can't stop thinking about it. "I picture it in my mind like a broken record. I just get kind of sick when I think about him inside her and his hands all over her. I worry when will she do it again and am I good enough in bed. I don't know why she cheated to be honest, other than the fact she wanted him from the minute she saw him, stating he was the best-looking man she had ever seen."

A characteristic of disgust is that it does not respond well to willpower. Disgust defines what we can admit to our body, and it guards the gates of our soul. It marks the line between what we welcome and what we find unacceptable. It pits our body and our mind against what we abhor.

When we are in love, we give permission to another to come closer than we permit anyone else. When that consent is violated, the barriers of disgust assert themselves without mercy. Our stomach is queasy, and we may vomit. As one British woman with an unfaithful husband put it to us, "I'm gutted."

We close this chapter with a vignette. A young woman is at home with her fiancé. One night, she picks up the phone and hears a woman's voice asking for her future husband. He takes the phone into their bedroom, an event so unusual she decides to listen in. She hears him say, "But wasn't last night special? I love you."

When she heard that, she told us, "I felt like I wanted to throw up." A moment later, looking out of the window in tears, she is overcome with rage. She slaps him harder than she thought she could ever hit anyone. Though he is eight inches taller, he cowers beneath her as she towers above. Enraged, she screams how she wasted a year of her life loving him. She is consumed by anger.

Understanding her anger is the point of the next chapter.

CHAPTER 3
ANGER

*"My attitude toward men who mess around is simple: If you
find 'em, kill 'em."*

—Loretta Lynn, country singer

*Last night, I was going through a bunch of old stuff when I came across a lock-
box. I had never seen it before and it was locked. There were keys hanging on a
hook. I found the key and opened it only to find a bunch of old love letters to
my husband. They covered eight or nine years and ended the year before we
married. In the box was a picture of a woman. She was black, and my husband
and I are white. I was shocked; I knew who this woman was. His parents
would have never approved of his goings on with a black woman.*

*I shut the box and went back to cleaning only to find another locked box. I
opened this one also, and in it were cards and letters dated through the first
fourteen years of our marriage. Once again they were from this same woman.
This time I was devastated to know he had been cheating with her almost our
entire married life. Her husband died three years ago. Now that she was finally
free, she assumed he would leave me for her, but he told her he would never do
that.*

*In her final letter to my husband, she wrote she felt used by him. She has
since remarried and moved to London. I also found a couple of cards from another woman covering the most recent four years of our marriage. She was
either having an affair with my husband or a very large infatuation.*

I lay awake in bed last night, wanting to kill my husband. I am so consumed with anger, hate, and disappointment. I wish nothing but ill will now for him and his whores. I don't know what to do. Has he truly ever loved me? In less than a year all our bills will be paid...

-Jane

Anger goes with being cheated on like jelly goes with peanut butter. The reason why is worth considering, because it goes straight to the reason this so-called irrational emotion is quite rational.

The Greek philosopher Aristotle considered each virtue a midpoint between two extremes, with one extreme representing too little of something and the other representing too much.[1] For example, courage is the midpoint between cowardice and recklessness, and friendliness is the midpoint between groveling and the grouch. And anger? In Aristotle's view anger is a midpoint between being hot-tempered and being a doormat.[2] He believed that anger is a virtue because it is our built-in, legitimate reaction to injustice. Anger prevents us from accepting rationalizations for wrongdoing, and it fuels our desire to see balance restored. It is, he believed, a point of excellence.

Aristotle also believed some acts are not examples of too much, too little, or just right; some things are bad in themselves. That is why, he explained, we can be angry at the right person to the right extent and in the right way, but there is no such thing as committing adultery with the right woman at the right time and in the right way.[3] At one point in his discussion of ethics, Aristotle groups adultery with desertion of a comrade in battle. At another, he groups it with sly acts like theft, poisoning, and procuring.[4]

Many people are taught to stifle their anger, but that is not quite right. What we must control are vengeance and violence. As advice givers, we never underestimate the potential for violence in any relationship. In the first year of our column we received a letter from a businessman on death row for murdering his wife. Another letter began with, "In [location and date] my husband was convicted of hiring a hit man to kill me." Some letters to us end with "Please do not print this. It would be very dangerous for me," or words to that effect, and we were not surprised when we got a letter from a woman saying, "...he got out a hunting rifle and threatened to kill me as well as my family."

There is always a potential for violence where cheating is involved. When one normally level-headed Canadian woman, working a humdrum civil service job, learned her boyfriend was cheating, she raced to his apartment. "I was so upset," she said, "I wanted to see him face-to-face. I needed to know why he treated me so badly." She called his cell phone to ask him to come out. He wouldn't answer, so she called his home phone. He wouldn't answer. She rang the doorbell, and he refused to come out. Then, she said, "I must have lost it." She smashed the passenger side window on his car, the mirrors on both sides, and the headlights, and carved LIAR into the hood. Afterward, she couldn't believe her actions. "I have never stooped to such stupidity before," she explained.

Violence can also appear as a defensive reaction from the cheater. When a woman told her boyfriend she had proof of his infidelity, "At first he chuckled then all of a sudden got this angry look in his eye. So I went to the front door to go on a walk and let him cool down. He came out after me and grabbed me by the hair. I screamed, and he dragged me into the house by my hair, threw me on the couch, then climbed on top of me and began choking me..."

One man became suspicious of a 'friend' his wife called incessantly. As the man went to call the friend's number, the wife took the phone out of his hand and smashed it over his head. She promised him, "If you ever embarrass me in front of my friends or interfere with my work, I will destroy your future..." Her friend, of course, was a man she was cheating with, and she was furious at being caught.

Infidelity carries with it the possibility of violence, even lethal violence, like murder or suicide. That threat requires taking precautions. But anger and violence are not the same thing. Violence seeks to destroy while anger, as a virtue, seeks fairness.

Fairness was on the minds of Sarah Brosnan and Frans de Waal when they conducted a modest experiment.[5] Brosnan, a biologist, and de Waal, a primatologist, taught capuchin monkeys how to exchange pebbles for food. In their experiment, two capuchins were placed side by side and took turns 'buying' identical rations of food with pebbles.

The experiment went smoothly until the experimenters turned the tables on the capuchins. Normally each monkey paid a pebble to 'buy' a slice of cucumber. Under the new rule, however, the first monkey paid with a pebble and got cucumber, while the second monkey paid with a pebble and got a grape. This mattered because, while capuchins like cucumbers, they love grapes. Not surprisingly, the monkeys who received a cucumber instead of a grape were miffed. They sulked or flung the pebbles and cucumber away.

Our desire for justice, fairness, and equity goes deep. As de Waal suggests, it is not something a clever human dreamed up on a rainy day. In his book Good Natured, he proposes our ancestors descended from animals that had been living in structured social communities for millions of years, and those communities survived only because they had rules governing right and wrong.[6] Those rules, like the rise of anger at injustice, are deeply embedded within us.

How deeply? Apparently as deep as our brain and our DNA. Three UCLA researchers—Golnaz Tabibnia, Ajay Satpute, and Matthew Lieberman—conducted experiments with the Ultimatum Game, a game used to examine how two people divide a sum of money.[7] In their version of the game, Person A received an unearned windfall of money, which they could divide however they chose with Person B. The catch was, if B didn't accept A's proposed division, neither person would get any money.

Sometimes A made B a fair offer, like $5 out of $10; other times the offer was unfair, like $5 out of $23. It was always to B's economic advantage to take the offer because he or she would end up with at least some money. But the experiment wasn't about fattening your wallet. It was about how humans react to unfairness, and those reactions were measured by hooking up people in the B position to a brain scan as they debated A's offer. What the experimenters learned was that brain reactions to fairness and unfairness are swift and automatic. Unfair offers quickly activate a region of the brain associated with moral disgust, while fair offers stimulate a brain region generally associated with getting rewards.

The capuchin and ultimatum game experiments point to another aspect of justice. Justice is not only about fairness, it is about empathy and sympathy. Someone who gives you the short end of the stick is more than unfair. They are unsympathetic. They do not identify with your feelings. They do not put themselves in your shoes. They are not at one with you. And that poses a question. Once you understand another person does not empathize with you, why would you go a step further and believe that person loves you? Love is a connector, and cheating says the connection to you doesn't go past the other's own desires.

A music producer in Los Angeles told us, just when he thought he found his soul mate, he had a major project back East. Three weeks into the new assignment, he flew his girlfriend in for a long weekend. It was fabulous. After she left, they stayed in touch through multiple daily phone calls and video chats. He counted the days until they could be in each other's arms again.

Upon his arrival back in LA, however, she seemed different. At first she said yes to a date then she changed her mind. "I'm kind of tired," she said. "Call me when you're done with work. You'll be done about 9:30, right?"

The music producer rushed to finish work early, jumped in his car in a torrential downpour, and raced up Interstate 405 to see her. Calling her from the road, there was no answer. He thought she probably fell asleep on her couch watching a movie as she said she was going to do. He called again, left a voicemail, and kept driving. He hoped to surprise her with a kiss and perhaps spend the night with the woman he loved.

As he pulled up to her house, all the lights were on. Definitely asleep on the couch, he thought. He knocked on the door. No answer. He knocked again. Still no answer. Turning to walk away, he heard the door unlock and expected to hear a sleepy, "Hi, baby. I dozed off. Oh, it's so sweet that you came over in this crazy rain just to see me!"

Instead she said, "Are you kidding me? You can't just drop by unannounced. I'm exhausted and I'm going to bed!" Looking down, he caught a reflection in a mirror. A man was sitting on the couch.

When she slammed the door, he felt like dropping to his knees, but his feelings quickly changed. "You bitch!" he yelled at her bay window then drove away screaming at her at the top of his lungs. It was, he said later, a "dumbass move."

In the Sermon on the Mount Jesus said, "Blessed are those who hunger and thirst for justice, for they shall be satisfied." Those words touch the essential feature of justice. Injustice creates a festering wound. When we are treated unfairly, we feel an unquenchable thirst, a thirst that will not be satisfied until the scales are balanced. Cheating, by its nature, is an imbalance, and by means conscious or otherwise we want to restore justice. Often, however, the methods we choose to restore justice make things worse.

A corporate pilot, married five years, had an affair in the third year of his marriage. His wife stayed but seethed with anger. Later, when he accepted a job with a female copilot, she threw a fit and forbade him to take it. He explained his goal was the major airlines, and he couldn't turn down a flight due his copilot's gender.

His wife was unmoved. She left their home, with the children, and became involved with another man. Eventually the pilot filed for divorce under "irreconcilable differences." She counter-filed under adultery. The adultery wasn't in question since the pilot freely admitted it, but that didn't matter to his wife. She wanted him publicly branded a cheater, and she vowed to subpoena his girlfriend as a way to even the score with both of them. This was the justice she sought.

I am 23 years old. My husband 'John' and I have been together for nearly four years. We always had problems, but we always managed to let things go and move on. Two years into our marriage, he cheated on me with a friend of mine. I got tired of it and left him. We got back together to try to work things out. We weren't sleeping together at first because I didn't want sex to be the basis of our reconciliation. During the first week back with John, I found out he was still seeing my ex-friend. I retaliated by cheating on him with one of his friends and got pregnant. Now, 22 months later, I have a beautiful one-year-old little boy who looks more and more like John's friend as he grows.

My husband and I both have green eyes, my son has blue. We are both short, my son is tall. We both have dark brown hair, my son is blond. Most people tell John that my son looks nothing like him and jokingly call him "the milkman's baby." And yet he has never put the pieces together.

John's friend is still around through email and social media, but I keep my son's pictures private so that neither of them will see the resemblance. To top it all off, we are currently living overseas so I am afraid if I tell John, he will want a divorce and I will be stuck in Japan with no way to get home. If I wait another two years, we will be back home in the U.S. And yet I know that he has a right to know and the longer I wait, the harder it will be on all of us. I'm not sure how to handle this. I feel guilty, but I am afraid of the outcome.

-Cathy

There are several lessons in Cathy's letter.

First, it shows what comes from taking a second bite at a wormy apple. "Everyone deserves a second chance" is a flawed belief, as the Marine officer in the last chapter found out when he married his cheating girlfriend. Second, the letter highlights the increasing use of DNA to prove parentage. Finally, it illustrates how dishonesty is like compound interest: its effects multiply over time.

But the aspect we want to focus on is retaliation.

The artist Julia Cameron was correct when she said, "Anger is meant to be acted upon."[8] But the form of that action needs to be effective. Distancing yourself from the offender can be effective; further involvement usually is not. After Cathy's husband cheated, she felt she had been sucker-punched. Her self-esteem was battered, and as he continued to cheat, she saw a reverse cheat as a misguided way to even the score.

We have received hundreds of letters involving the reverse or revenge cheat. Sometimes the payback happens quickly, but often, as in the letter below, retribution is taken years later.

I have male friends who are just friends, but my husband is so insecure about them it is driving me crazy. A year ago, at Christmas, he took our children to visit family out of town. I could not go because of work. While my family was gone, I invited a male friend to go to Christmas Eve service with me. I told my husband, and he had no reaction.

Six months later, my spouse complained I was spending too much time with other men. He insisted I have one of the children with me to act as a chaperone. A chaperone for what I do not know, because nothing ever happens. We live in a small town with nosey neighbors who report my comings and goings to my husband. These neighbors must lead such boring and miserable lives, they try to make my life as miserable as theirs.

My husband claims I disrespected him by taking a friend to church when he wasn't home. Wouldn't it have been more disrespectful if I had not told him? Nine years ago, he had an affair with a woman in our home. I feel he's carrying around guilt about the affair and laying it onto me, which is not fair. I have been in therapy for a year now. My husband has gone to the last two sessions with me. I discovered he married me because he felt 'obligated' since we had sex before marriage. No, I was not pregnant.

In twenty years I have never been unfaithful, and I don't plan to be, but I can't go on much longer with my husband not trusting me. This has driven a big wedge between us. My therapist says everyone deserves friends, whether they be male or female. Any advice?

-Susan

Susan's husband thinks, as many cheaters do, "She's no better than me. If I would cheat, she would cheat." But on a subconscious level his wife's contact with other men may be an exquisitely slow payback for his affair nine years before. It is like pricking him with a pin, again and again.

Another woman found a different way of taking revenge. "I thought maybe we could be happy again if I found a way to even the score, but I didn't do it by cheating on him. You see, we are both in the military, and adultery in the military can be punished under Article 134, the General Article. It forbids conduct bringing discredit on the armed forces or prejudicial to good order and discipline. So I turned him in. His punishment included forfeiture of pay, 14 extra duty days, and a black mark on his career."

People who talk about infidelity in terms of right and wrong are often accused of being 'moralistic,' as if they hold an absurd belief they are trying to impose on others. Or they are accused of "black and white thinking." But when we say infidelity is wrong, we reference not personal belief but principles derived from reasoning and research.

An elderly man told us he arrived at army boot camp in the early days of the Second World War. One evening, he and the other fellows sat around debating morality. One recruit said, when he wondered if something was right or wrong, he always asked himself, "What if everybody did it?" If everybody did it and the result was bad, the recruit said, he concluded the action was wrong.

Unknowingly, this soldier had hit upon philosopher Immanuel Kant's first maxim: act only in a way which wills that your act becomes a universal law. Applying this to cheating yields the following result. If everyone cheated, then honesty could not exist and justice as a concept would not exist. Nobody could be trusted. The social order would be chaos.

A woman told us her husband's affair with a coworker began with meetings at a convenience store. They sat and talked in their cars. The coworker was, his wife wrote, "my age, but a little thinner, not pretty, just someone who noticed him and made him feel good about himself." The wife learned of the affair when the other woman's husband called and said he had 10 motel receipts to prove his wife and her husband were cheating together. One receipt was from a town south of where they lived and the other nine from a town in the north.

When she asked her husband why he went so many times to a motel in the north and then suddenly to one in the south, his mouth dropped wide open. He was livid. "I never went there," he cried. The other woman apparently was involved with two men and pinned it all on him. After her husband's affair ended, the writer said she couldn't handle the pain. Two and a half years later, they divorced. After two more years passed, they remarried, which sometimes happens when neither divorced person finds another partner.

She continued, "He said he made a mistake, that he was weak, that he loved me and wanted to be with me. I have to admit he has been really good to me since the affair came out." But she cannot get over the details. The things he did with the other woman keep popping into her head and making her angry. She even tried hypnosis to block it all out, but the "memories rear their ugly heads."

She lamented, "I used to say that I would die for him. I would not say that now." She asks us how to overcome the awful pain she goes through almost on a daily basis and says, "I am so scared to trust him with the rest of my life."

She has good reason to be afraid to trust him. That is why suspicion is the focus of the next chapter.

CHAPTER 4
SUSPICION

"Not that you lied to me, but that I no longer believe you, has shaken me."

—Friedrich Nietzsche, philosopher

I never thought I would be in need of advice from anyone on relationships. I always thought myself very good at dealing with problems. However, I am having a great deal of trouble letting go of the past. It started about one year ago. My girlfriend, Blake, whom I had been dating for almost a year, began acting distant. I knew something wasn't right and confronted her, and for three months she insisted nothing was going on.

-Keith

Eventually Blake admits she's been physically involved with an ex-boyfriend. She excuses her actions by saying she wasn't ready to let go of him as a friend, and it was merely sex done from a sense of obligation.

Needless to say, Keith goes on,

I felt completely betrayed. I thought I had found the perfect woman. It has been nine months since the big revelation, and I am no better off than I was when I first found out. I can't seem to begin to trust her again. I don't know how to let this heal. Though she does say she will never break up with me and will stay as long as it takes for me to feel good about us again, I'm afraid that day won't come. How can I forget the awful past and move on to better things?

When people ask us how to overcome the nagging suspicions raised by a cheating partner, they ask the wrong question. "How do I get over this?" is what they ask. A better question is, "What basis in fact is there to believe I will ever get over this?"

Some years ago, psychologists Myron Rothbart and Bernadette Park created a list of 150 human traits.[1] These traits were described using words like messy, adventurous, boring, and heroic. Eight words on their list involved trust. Those words were boastful, deceitful, phony, deceptive, untruthful, truthful, honest, and trustworthy. Rothbart and Park then asked people how easy it is to prove or disprove the existence of each trait in another person.

What they found is that trust-related traits are unique in requiring large numbers of instances to establish and few instances to disprove. As Paul Slovic, a psychologist and expert on decision making, says, trust follows an asymmetry principle.[2] It is hard to build, easy to destroy, and leaves suspicion behind in its wake.

A woman told us her husband of three years was having an affair with a girl in the next subdivision. He confessed to her only after the other woman came to their house to talk to the wife. The question this wife asked us was simple. "How do I get past the pain? I hurt all the time and don't trust him anymore. I used to kiss him goodbye and tell him to be safe as he left me home alone to go cheat with her. I don't want to keep bringing this up with him, but I am absolutely torn in half over this. How do you learn to let go of the pain?"

That question—how do you learn to let go of the pain?—hides other questions. The two we want to address in this chapter are: Where does the pain come from and why is it there in the first place?

Leda Cosmides, a psychologist, and John Tooby, an anthropologist, have focused their careers on investigating the human past to understand the workings of the mind. One of their main findings is that the mind is

32

not an all-purpose machine. Rather, different neural circuits are special-ized for different problems.[3] These neural circuits are designed to solve problems our ancestors faced. Specifically, these are problems that recur and are so threatening we need to solve them correctly the first time we run into them.

One such problem is how to deal with cheaters. Humans and their ancestors have been living in social situations for, to pick a round number, two million years. That's two million years of swapping and bartering, trading and exchanging, talking and discussing (or maybe gesturing and grunting in the beginning). To live together successfully, rules evolved which govern social exchange.

What Cosmides and Tooby and other researchers demonstrated is that within our minds is a highly evolved mechanism for detecting cheat-ers. Over the long reach of human history this has proved beneficial. So much is this true that every normal person on the planet today possesses a program that says, if you take a benefit, then you must fulfill the condition under which the benefit was given. People who violate this rule are called cheaters.

The rule simply says, if A, then B.[4] What's interesting is that when this statement is presented as an abstract logical problem, people typically fail to reach the correct conclusion. We don't reason very well. But when the rule involves a social exchange between people, we understand with a high degree of accuracy if we've been cheated. In short, something in our brain has specialized itself as a cheater detection system.

Further experiments show this system only goes off when someone intentionally wants to cheat.[5] If a person gets an unearned benefit by acci-dent or with an innocent intention, or if someone gets an unearned benefit but it doesn't benefit them, the cheater alarm system is silent.

As you might expect, Harvard undergraduates do well on tests of de-tecting cheaters in social situations.[6] What's far more interesting is that the Shiwiar, hunter-horticulturalists in the remote Ecuadorian Amazon, do just as well as kids at Harvard. So do people in Europe, Hong Kong, the United States, Japan and apparently everywhere else.

This line of research established that we have, in our brains, a sophisticated system for detecting cheaters. More surprisingly, research has shown this ability to detect cheaters is found in children by the age of three of four. Preschoolers can do it, and preschoolers in all cultures can do it. Preschoolers also understand the difference between intentional and accidental cheating.

Astoundingly, people with schizophrenia, who have extreme shortfalls in brain function, may maintain the ability to detect cheaters. In other words, our cheater detection program can remain intact even when our general reasoning ability is damaged. The overall conclusion of Cosmides and Tooby is this ability is not learned. It is within us by virtue of being human. It is universal.

That leads us back to the two questions we started with. Where does the pain of betrayal come from? And why is it there in the first place? The answers are the pain comes from our cheater detection system and it is there because dealing with cheaters has proven over the course of human history to be perilous.

We have a system that sounds an alarm in our brain when we detect cheating. It is innate. The problem for those who think they can stay with a cheater is how do you live with a danger signal constantly ringing in your mind and body?

We would like to offer an easy answer, but there is no easy answer. Instead, we will give you the honest answer. No one knows. As Paul Ekman, the expert on facial expression and deception, said, "A big cost of lying is people won't be able to trust you again...nobody knows the ability it takes to reestablish trust. You can't work with someone, let alone live with someone, if you don't trust them."[7]

The truth of that statement is illustrated in the following letter:

I have been with an amazing man for the past year. Our relationship is complicated, as we commenced dating off and on eight years ago. It only lasted two years because I cheated on him...twice. I told him the truth the next day because I have an enormous conscience and thought if I told him the truth, I would be forgiven.

I'm not sure why this occurred and rationalize it due to the fact that I was young and stupid and didn't know what I had. Now we are trying this again as we feel we are meant to be together. The only problem is he is having a difficult time getting over the fact that I cheated so many years ago.

He has been given the opportunity to cheat on me over the past number of months, and it makes him sick to even think about being with someone else. To the point he thinks of me, and how I could let it happen, which makes him hate me for a split second. Then he rationalizes and admits he loves me.

-Valerie

We aren't sure whether Valerie understood what she was saying when she called her boyfriend's gut reaction hate and his "I love you" a rationalization, but she got it right.

The cheating rule embedded within us is simple. It says, if you take a benefit, you must fulfill the condition under which the benefit was given. If you take my love, you must be faithful. It's a good rule. It prevents exploitation. As Cosmides and Tooby point out, it solves a well-defined problem in a well-defined way. If I give you this, you give me that.

In an evolutionary sense, perhaps our ancestors tried out two mental programs. One said help without receiving in return. The other said help under one condition: the one you help must return the favor. People who followed the first program would have become extinct. Only those who helped on a reciprocal basis would have survived because only that program allows both parties to be better off after an exchange.

Variations of the rule appear everywhere. They are found in every legal system. To cite just one example, a health care statute in the United

States defines fraud as *a knowing and willful deception, or misrepresentation, or reckless disregard of facts, with the intent to receive an unauthorized bene-fit.*[8] That's the evolutionary rule. Precisely.

Broken trust leaves long-lasting suspicion as its residue, which is why business people won't stay in business with a partner or employee who embezzles. It is why nations never forgive traitors. Though whistleblow-ers' acts are often to protect or warn, a cloud of suspicion hangs over even them. They make us uncomfortable. Our cheater detection system thrums in their presence. It senses something akin to, but not identical with, what it was designed to detect.

After an infidelity, suspicion becomes a way of life for the victim. He's late returning from work. Where is he? Who is he meeting? Why is she wearing that outfit to work? Who is she wearing it for? If he answers the phone and walks out of the room, who is he talking to? What plans are they making? Should I go through her emails, phone, or purse?

In this chapter and the two previous ones, we focused on the three specific things left in the wake of cheating—disgust, anger, and suspicion, which is the loss of trust. However, betrayal kicks up much more, an array of things difficult to label. This array includes intrusive thoughts, feelings of hopelessness, lack of confidence, depression, insomnia, headaches, and nervous stomach. These things go by a different name: trauma.

Trauma is the fourth major impact of betrayal on the victim, and it is the subject of the next chapter.

CHAPTER 5

TRAUMA

"I pray as often as I feel helpless, and God seems not to hear."
—Anonymous writer

That line is from a 3500-word, handwritten letter sent to us by a man in Latin America. His words describe the despair he feels married to an unfaithful woman. He concluded his letter by writing, "May God NEVER allow my life to be repeated in any of my children's lives."

A woman reports her husband started dating another woman and "My side of the bed hasn't even had a chance to cool off yet.... I am experiencing the same type of pain that I had when my oldest son was killed. I am so devastated. I always thought he was the love of my life. I feel so betrayed and used. My self-esteem is at an all-time low. I feel so inadequate, unattractive, and hopeless. How does someone overcome these feelings and get back into living?"

Betrayal is a stressful event far beyond our normal, everyday experience. Those words—a stressful event far beyond our normal, everyday experience—form the textbook definition of trauma. Trauma shatters our worldview. It attacks our confidence. It floods us with images, emotions, and thoughts we can't let go of. Unless we find a way to heal, the suffering remains present in our lives, even after decades.

When two Canadian researchers, Stephen Porter and Kristine Peace, conducted an experiment on memory, they discovered that traumatic memories differ from ordinary memories.[1] Ordinary, positive emotional memories, created by what we see, touch, taste, hear, or smell, deteriorate dramatically in vividness, quality, and sensory elements over time. The picture fades. But traumatic memories are factually consistent over long periods of time. Their vividness and quality remain essentially unchanged. Porter and Peace concluded that trauma creates scars on our memory, making it unlike normal memory, which grows steadily fainter.

The story of a man who wrote us a few years ago illustrates this well. He wasn't, he said, the typical husband who abandons his wife to watch TV. He and his wife did everything—cards, movies, or what have you—together.

She loved steamed crabs and beer, and though it was expensive on their budget, he would get them for her on almost a daily basis. When she seemed a little down, he would take her to a hotel because she loved staying in hotels. They were both religious, and he tried to follow Paul's biblical command to men: love your wife as you love yourself.

When the kids were growing up and attending school, his wife returned to work. He noticed she began mentioning one man's name a lot but didn't think much of it because she was gregarious by nature. A few months later, when she complained he wasn't affectionate enough, he promised to work on it. He thought if it were true, it was because earlier in their marriage she had pushed him away many times. Still, he began to tell her often how much he loved her.

Though she was not normally a phone person, he noticed she was now on her phone a lot. She claimed it was a female friend from work, but when she was on the phone with this friend, she would leave the room, and if the kids were in the vicinity, she told them to go away. As she grew more secretive, he became more troubled and inquisitive.

One day, he placed a mini-recorder in her car. When he retrieved it—this was on Super Bowl Sunday—he got the shock of his life. The device recorded his wife's conversation with a girlfriend about the affair the wife was having with a coworker. She was upset that her male coworker wanted to break it off because *he* felt bad for being unfaithful to *his* girlfriend.

When the husband confronted his wife, she lied and said they just talked. He played the tape, and she admitted she 'manipulated' the other man just once. With each retelling, a few more details came out until she admitted she performed oral sex on the other man at least four times. He wrote us,

To imagine her sucking on his penis was just unimaginable. To add to this was the fact that she didn't have him use protection and she would kiss me afterward...

I have never been a depressed person, but now I am. I never thought that I was a handsome person, but I never felt ugly. I KNOW I am ugly. I haven't accomplished a lot in life, but I always prided myself on my marriage and family, so much so that others would come to me for advice. So now I have nothing.

I'm not an emotional guy, but now, over a year later, I can cry at anything. A nonstop DVD in my head continued to play scenes of him and her having sex or detailed things she told me about them. My feeling for her left the day I found out. I reasoned it would come back, but it didn't. This feeling continued to increase, and finally I separated from her and filed for divorce.

I can't say I don't have feelings for my wife. My feelings are anger. I know many articles on the internet said this would subside, but it only subsided within me when I separated. They have also said that an affair is the same as every other way that we fail each other in a marriage.

I could take every hurt and wrong from my wife and pile them up and they would still be a molehill compared to the mountain I am under after this affair. I know what the experts say, but it would never have been the same!! Never! I know all the experts say that something was lacking, but I go over and over and over this in my head...

And he can't find anything else he should have done.

Scalding water reddens the skin, malnutrition makes muscle waste away, and a fall from a high place will break your bones. In the same way, exposure to trauma has predictable after-effects. Traumatic events would stress anyone because they are a fundamental attack on our person. When we suffer trauma, our reaction says little about us as individuals and much about the nature of the human organism.

Traumatic events trigger physical, emotional, mental, and social repercussions in the victim, but there is no clear dividing line between these spheres. They interact in a way which is seamless, and the symptoms can appear in almost any combination.

On the physical level trauma may cause rapid heartbeat, higher blood pressure, stomach and intestinal disorders, diarrhea, headache, restlessness, insomnia, nightmares, excessive sleep, chronic fatigue, chest pain, backache, and panic attacks.

On an emotional level trauma can cause despair, apathy, fear, anxiety, overeating, and the use of alcohol or drugs to blunt memory. It produces feelings of powerlessness, deadening of the emotions, and loss of self-worth. Feelings of humiliation and shame, as well as emotional flooding, are common.

On a mental level trauma can produce anger directed at oneself (thoughts of self-harm) or anger directed at others (violence). It produces intrusive recall, lack of concentration, and loss of trust in others and in the world. Feelings of hopelessness, abandonment, and grief are common. Ideas and images pass through the mind without being processed. The traumatized person is unable to imagine life getting better.

On a social level trauma results in the inability to do daily tasks, withdrawal from the world, and disruption of one's career. Because victims are often afraid to tell others what happened, they become socially isolated. The victim relives the past, is unable to stay in the present, and loses interest in what they normally enjoy.

Many trauma experts believe our ability to recover from traumatic shock is related to the source of the shock. Glenn Schiraldi, the author of *The Post-Traumatic Stress Disorder Sourcebook*, divides the causes of trauma into three categories: natural events, man-made but unintentional events, and man-made intentional events.[2] Natural events are things like tornados, volcanic eruptions, and earthquakes. Man-made, unintentional events include a crane toppling, a skywalk collapsing, or a plane crashing. Schiraldi's final category—man-made, deliberate events—includes exposure to things like incest, trench warfare, and stalking.

As a general rule, experts agree that natural disasters are the easiest events to get past. It's hard to stay mad at Mother Nature. The next easiest traumas to overcome are man-made, unintentional events. Though they may be bad and even tragic in their consequences, the lack of a deliberate intent to harm makes them easier to accept.

The hardest events to overcome are those which are man-made and deliberate. Cheating adds one additional element to that. Not only was the act man-made, not only was it deliberate, it was done by a person within our smallest circle of attachment. We believed they cared for us. We believed they loved us. When they violated our safe haven, it destroyed our belief that we are the one for them and they the one for us. Victims of cheating often feel, "Before, I believed it was us against the world; now I realize I am alone."

An oddity of trauma is that victims often blame themselves for what happened, even though what happened was beyond their control. This is true regardless of the source of the trauma.

Psychotherapist Babette Rothschild, a specialist in trauma recovery, tells about a woman who planned a family vacation in the Indian Ocean.[3] As luck would have it, she planned it for December 2004 in the area where a tsunami was about to kill over a quarter of a million people. The event was a natural disaster, impossible to predict. Her family was simply in the wrong place at the wrong time. Yet, characteristic of trauma survivors, this woman couldn't stop blaming herself for putting her family at risk, even though they all survived. As Rothschild recounts in her book *8 Keys to Safe Trauma Recovery*, she couldn't let go of those feelings until the day her teenage son yelled, "Stop it, Mom! Who do you think you are? God? Only God knew that was going to happen. IT WAS NOT YOUR FAULT!"

Al Haynes was a United Airlines captain on a flight from Denver to Chicago when his DC-10 suffered the simultaneous failure of three separate, redundant hydraulic systems after an engine exploded.[4] The crew lost all control mechanisms on the aircraft, and the crippled plane kept trying to roll on its back at 35,000 feet. The aircraft lurched up and down in the sky like a porpoise. Even worse, the jet could only turn right.

Yet, 44 minutes later, the crew brought the plane to the site of the nearest airport, Sioux City, Iowa. With incredible skill and timing, the pilot and crew lined the plane up with the center of the runway just as the jetliner was completing another 360-degree circle. They lost what little control they had short of the runway. One hundred and twelve people died in the crash, but 184 survived.

Later, at the United Airlines training facility in Denver, 57 flight crews were placed in simulators in the identical situation.[5] Not one crew was able to control the plane to the runway, and most of them lost control in midair. Safety investigators, who usually find fault with a crew, concluded it was impossible to guide such a crippled plane to an airfield. Yet Al Haynes and his crew did it. So extraordinary was their effort that the wife of a man who died thanked Haynes for his valor in giving her husband at least a chance at survival.[6]

Yet Al Haynes could not shake the feeling he had been at fault.[7] He continued to fly for United for two years until his mandatory retirement. In retirement he gave a hundred speeches a year, never accepting a fee, on traumatic stress and other issues surrounding disaster. As he said, "Every time I give it...I convince myself just a little bit more that there was nothing else I could do."

Trauma is caused by things which overtake us, and traumatic events by definition are beyond our control. As psychotherapist Babette Rothschild points out, if you could have done something about it, it wouldn't have been a trauma.

That raises a question. Why do we blame ourselves for things beyond our control?

An experiment by Wellesley College psychologist Linda Carli provides one answer.[8] Carli had people read descriptions of an encounter between a man and a woman. In this story a woman meets a man, her boss, for dinner. Afterward the couple goes to his home and has a glass of wine. Then the man leads the woman to the couch, takes her hand, and asks her to marry him. It's a happy ending. Or at least it was for half the people who read the story. The other half read an identical story with the opposite result. In this ending the man pushes the woman onto the couch, pins her down, and rapes her. Interestingly, those who read the happy ending found no fault with the woman's behavior or character, while those who read the other ending blamed the woman and saw the rape as inevitable.

Carli's story illustrates hindsight bias, which is a characteristic of our mind. From outcomes we draw conclusions. We do this despite all evidence to the contrary, and we do it even though at the outset we are totally unable to predict what will happen. Most of us grow up with the idea that if we are good, good things will happen to us. But that isn't true. Much of life is unfair and unpredictable. However, self-blame gives us the illusion of control, and the idea that we can control events is comforting. That may be why the woman blamed herself for her family being caught in a tsunami. It is why some victims of cheating blame themselves.

It is unfortunate that trauma victims blame themselves for events, but we know it is simply a characteristic of surviving neurological trauma.

What's worse is when others, partly applying hindsight bias and partly because of an unconscious belief it could never happen to them, blame the victim. What is important to remember about trauma is this indisputable fact. Trauma victims often blame themselves though they are blameless.

Unfortunately, some therapists appear to use that fact to maneuver the betrayed person into taking responsibility for what happened. Sometimes the victim is asked to "take your part in this" or "acknowledge your role." Questions may be posed, such as, "What did you contribute to your partner's dissatisfaction?" or "What qualities do you have that make you at fault?" or "What needs of your partner did you fail to respond to?" However it is phrased, the victim is asked to "accept your fair share of responsibility" for what happened.

We repeat; it is a known fact of trauma that victims tend to blame themselves for what happened. In our view, any psychological helper or clergy member who uses that fact to steer the betrayed person into assuming blame for someone else's cheating borders on unethical conduct. This tactic also plays into the hands of the cheater, who is often only too happy to lay blame on their partner. Our advice is to be extremely leery of anyone who suggests your partner's cheating is your fault.

Trauma is assessed in a number of ways, and these ways usually involve recall or structured interviews. Both the International Society for Traumatic Stress Studies and the U.S. Veterans Administration consider one test the "gold standard" in trauma assessment.[9] It is called the CAPS test (Clinician Administered PTSD Scale).

The CAPS test is used to assess trauma over a week, a month, or a lifetime. In its traditional version, it assesses the frequency and intensity of symptoms in three areas: re-experiencing symptoms, avoidance and numbing symptoms, and hyperarousal symptoms.[10] Re-experiencing symptoms include things like intrusive recall and distressing dreams.

Avoidance and numbing symptoms include steering clear of people, places, and activities, as well as unplugging from feelings as a way to reduce pain. Hyperarousal symptoms include problems falling or staying asleep and difficulty in concentration. In hyperarousal, ideas pass through the mind like a runaway train.

The CAPS test is designed to be administered by a trained person. However, as of this writing, it can be found online. While we do not recommend self-diagnosis, it can be useful for people who have been cheated on to look over this or similar measures of trauma, so they have an idea what they are dealing with. Most victims of betrayal who write us describe symptoms of serious trauma in their letters. Often, they are unaware they are describing traumatic stress.

Treatment of traumatic stress is a psychological specialty. It does not involve or include the person who caused the trauma. If you know or believe your trauma is at a significant level, you may want to consider treatment because, as someone said, trauma is not something you can think your way out of.

The classic view of trauma goes something like this:[11] A traumatic event occurs and seriously disturbs a person's life. Once the event is over, a period of safety follows. The tornado victim is taken to a hospital, the soldier is removed from the front lines, the floodwaters recede and the Red Cross arrives with food, water, and temporary shelter. The trauma victim suffers the effects of the trauma, but he or she is removed from the source of the harm.

At that point, in two wonderfully ambiguous words psychologists use, the victim must "process" and "integrate" the traumatic event. This is the fork in the road. Either the person will remain stuck with traumatic symptoms or they will get past them and find harmony within themselves. If they achieve a lasting calm, the event no longer triggers recurring symptoms. If they don't, they remain chronic victims. The event still makes them anxious; they have recurring memories, images, emotions, and physical symptoms. They stay stuck in dysfunction.

But if the source of the trauma is betrayal and the victim stays with the person who betrayed them, there is no period of safety. The Red Cross never arrives. The shell-shocked soldier is stuck in a trench at the front. The victim is moored to the site of the trauma, which may make the trauma impossible to overcome.

One woman told us she found evidence of her husband's affair when she checked his cell phone. When she confronted him, he admitted it. Then she made him move into a hotel. The following day, his girlfriend, who was his employee, told the husband she didn't want to be party to a messy divorce and was content to stay with her boyfriend. Two days later, the wife allowed her husband to come home.

After he came home, she tried everything. As she says, "We have been involved in a marriage support group, we both go to counseling, which is costing us a fortune, and I go to a support group myself. My whole life is consumed by his affair. All the books say it just takes time, but when I read your article about infidelity, it is just what I feel. He got dumped by his girlfriend, got to come home and have his family back, and I am sentenced for life with his affair."

I am sentenced for life with his affair sums up thousands of letters we have received from those who stayed.

Previously we mentioned an ethical problem faced by psychological and religious helpers who encourage the victim of cheating to stay. Because trauma victims often blame themselves when they are blameless, it is ethically and morally wrong to tell them to take responsibility for what their partner chose to do.

There is a second ethical question for these therapists and clergy. It goes without saying victims need a place of safety after suffering trauma. In fact, one standard practice in helping trauma victims to recover is to remind them they are in a different place from where the trauma occurred.[12] In light of what is known about trauma and recovery from trauma, why would anyone suggest the victim stay with their betrayer at the site of the victimization? What generally accepted psychological principles or moral principles justify that view? In what way does that satisfy the known standards for treating trauma victims?

These two serious ethical issues—blaming the victim and not encouraging them to move to safety—are seldom, if ever, discussed in books on cheating. If the two parties are married, there is yet another problem. A marriage contract has been breached by one party resulting in serious injury to the other party. Telling the victim to stay because of a piece of paper is like telling the shell-shocked soldier he must go back to the front because he signed an enlistment contract.

"I am one big load of feces walking around," a man told us, describing how degrading it feels to be cheated upon. Cheating inflicts deep emotional wounds. In the past four chapters we summarized those wounds under the categories of disgust, anger, suspicion, and trauma. What would be helpful now is to look at this wounding in a broader context, the context of emotion in general.

That's a tall order. The emotions have been discussed and written about for thousands of years, and no one theory adequately explains them. That said, there are two things we would like you to remember about the emotions. Those two things are the subject of the next chapter.

CHAPTER 6
THE EMOTIONS

"When we listen to our emotions, we are not being swayed by meaningless feelings... We are using our bodies to perceive our position in the world."

—Jesse Prinz, philosopher of the mind

Early in the 20th century, it was thought that emotions vary from culture to culture and are learned.[1] Today, it is hard to find many who believe that. Now researchers believe emotions are universal, with only minor cultural variations.

Many of us grew up with the obsolete Western notion that human beings are basically minds riding around on top of bodies. It is the view that holds, as Cosmides and Tooby say, that emotions are merely the "goo that clogs the gearwheels of reasoning."[2]

Jon Haidt, a moral psychologist, describes that outmoded theory as the story of a dog and its tail.[3] Traditionally reason was considered the dog and emotions the tail. Haidt believes the opposite is true. Our values come from our feelings, not from a cold process of abstract reasoning. As Haidt says, "...moral emotions and intuitions drive moral reasoning, just as surely as a dog wags its tail."

Emotion provides the value, and reason trudges behind finding grounds to justify what we feel. Because moral judgments are made instantaneously, it suggests that conscious reasoning is not the primary factor. When someone cheats on you, a combination of emotion appears spontaneously. It tells you in a flash how to interpret the event.

Yet many people still believe emotion simply interferes with reason and reason can be used to stifle legitimate emotion. That's a problem with the traditional model of "getting past infidelity". It is built on the premise that we can use an overlay of thinking to overcome our embedded emotional structure.

As neuroscientist and cardiologist Alan Watkins says, our sense of self ebbs and flows with our emotions.[4] Wrapped in negative emotion, our sense of self and our consciousness shrink. We feel less than we were before. Welling up with positive emotion, our sense of self and awareness expand. We are worthy; we can do anything; life is good. What is beyond dispute is that emotions are states of feeling, which may be long-term and persistent, and they include physical and physiological changes that influence our thinking and our behavior.

Personality psychologist David Watson calls each emotion "an organized, highly structured reaction to an event that is relevant to the needs, goals, or survival" of an organism.[5] Each emotion, he says, includes a prototypical form of expression (like a facial expression), a pattern of consistent autonomic changes (like changes in heart rate and respiration), a distinct feeling state (like being scared witless), and a characteristic form of adaptive behavior (like wanting to run like hell).

Practically speaking, we find it useful to think of the emotions as cognitive programs that activate as needed, something like a smoke detector in our home.

We have received thousands of letters from people who have been cheated on, and the most impressive thing is the consistency in their response to cheating. We now summarize that response as DAST, a convenient acronym that holds the symptoms, and what they represent, together:

DAST
Disgust - revulsion
Anger - injustice
Suspicion - lack of trust, fear
Trauma - profound disruption of body and mind

If you have been cheated on, you may be miserable, but your feelings are exactly what they should be for someone in your situation. Your mind and body are working perfectly. They are working in a way honed by millions of years of evolution, or, if you prefer, by God's design.

At the end of the last chapter we asked you to remember two main points about the emotions. The first is that our emotions give us values that guide us, values like love and disgust, fairness and unfairness, trust and suspicion. The second point is, if you've been cheated on, your brain has generated the response befitting your position. If we would add a third point, it is this. The emotions surrounding cheating cannot be easily extinguished. So much is this the case that they can pop out full force, years or decades later, if you stay with a cheater.

The DAST emotions come from the architecture of the human mind, or, more exactly, the architecture of the entire human being. Trying to overcome disgust, anger, suspicion, and trauma by staying with a cheater is sledding uphill. Looking at cheating from a coldly rational perspective, a penis and a vagina came together and neither one belonged to me. That's all. But, oh, what a difference it makes to us.

The lesson from disgust, anger, suspicion, and trauma is that in order to stay with a cheater, you must defeat your own biology, and when we say biology here, we mean the totality of your being.

This chapter has been about feelings. In the next chapter we turn away from the emotions and address the topic of risk. Risk is a field that serves up answers with near mathematical precision. That sounds like risk has nothing to do with feelings, but that isn't the case. Risk often tells us things we'd rather not hear.

CHAPTER 7

RISK

"Prediction, not narration, is the real test of our understanding of the world."

—Nassim Nicholas Taleb, essayist

One book on staying together after infidelity shows a rope stretched horizontally across the cover. The rope is taut, but it has been cut and the two ends tied together in a crude knot. Will the rope hold? Would you try to tow a car or lift a piano with that rope? Would you trust it with your life? Those are the questions in this chapter.

In 1982, two researchers, Amos Tversky and Daniel Kahneman, published a paper about what is known as "The Linda Problem."[1] Tversky and Kahneman gave people a one-paragraph description of a woman and asked them to draw conclusions. This is the paragraph:

"Linda is 31 years old, single, outspoken, and very bright. She majored in philosophy. As a student she was deeply concerned with issues of discrimination and social justice, and also participated in antinuclear demonstrations."

Readers were asked which is more likely:

- Linda is a bank teller.
- Linda is a bank teller and active in the feminist movement.

Almost 90% of those tested thought it most likely that Linda was a bank teller and a feminist. That's the wrong answer, and it is wrong for a simple reason. The occurrence of two events cannot be more likely than the occurrence of a single event. Each time we add a new element, the likelihood of finding it in company with another element goes down.

It's a little like asking, are you more likely to find a pair of shoes in a store or a pair of shoes and a banjo? Is it more likely to find a pair of shoes in a store or a pair of shoes, a banjo, and a puppy?

But what does this have to do with infidelity? A lot, as it turns out. If you are deciding whether to stay with a cheater, try making a list beginning with what happened. Then add what you would like to see happen. For example, one person's list might look like this:

- My partner cheated.
- My partner cheated, is staying with me.
- My partner cheated, is staying with me, is sorry.
- My partner cheated, is staying with me, is sorry, is now honest.
- My partner cheated, is staying with me, is sorry, is now honest, won't do it again.
- My partner cheated, is staying with me, is sorry, is now honest, won't do it again, I'll get over it.

There are other things you might add to the list, but the important thing to remember is this. The more you wish for, the less likely you are to get it. As the amount of detail increases, the chance of getting those details decreases. With each item you add, the odds of achieving what you want go down. If you want 10 things, the odds are worse than wanting nine things. Wanting five things, the odds are worse than wanting four things. Wanting two things, the odds are worse than wanting one thing.

Yet, oddly enough, the more elaborate the description of an event, the more likely we are to believe it.[2] To put it another way, we are suckers for a good story.

For example, in one experiment, a group of people were given a scenario about a slightly shady businessman in the import/export business.[3] Then they were asked the probability of the businessman's involvement in various activities, including murder. For half the members of the group, the murder was described as killing an employee. For the other half, the murder was described as killing an employee to keep him from talking to the police. Again, the more detailed story was thought more plausible, even though it includes only a single scenario, while the murder could have occurred for many other reasons.

Now consider this story. A couple stays together after one party's infidelity. We might add details such as she cheated because he wasn't giving her enough attention or he cheated because he was thrown together with another woman at work. Now we have created a richer, more detailed story. We might even add that after infidelity they built a wonderful relationship. But the added details are not evidence. Though they add causality and motivation, they add nothing to probability. We-got-over-his-or-her-infidelity-to-build-a-wonderful-relationship is a great story. But a second story, one of them cheated yet they stayed together, is far more likely.

Ask people what they think about something and what generally bubbles to the surface is not a product of thought but something in memory.[4] That something, passed off as an opinion, might be from a movie, a novel, or a homily, and the mere fact of recalling an instance makes people want to count it as evidence. If you were exposed to a couple 'overcoming' infidelity in a film, story, or homily, you might believe it is possible, but all you are doing is retrieving a story from memory. That leads us to a key point made by risk expert Glynis Breakwell in her book *The Psychology of Risk*.[5] How you represent risks to yourself, and the actual amount of risk present, may have nothing to do with each other.

Risk is about hazards, and a hazard is anything that can hurt you.[6] Risk is also about harm, and harm is assessed in two ways: first, by the likelihood you will be harmed, and second, by the severity of the harm if it occurs.

What are the odds of a flu outbreak? Will the dam break? Should we release a violent criminal from prison? Those questions belong to the first part of risk assessment—the odds a harm will happen. The second part of risk assessment asks about the severity of the harm. How bad will the flu outbreak be? What will happen to those downstream from the dam? Will releasing the felon end in tragedy? It is a truism among those in the field of risk management that a risk cannot be managed until it has been assessed. That is why insurance companies, hospitals, businesses, schools, and governments all use risk assessment. They can't predict the future, but they need to make the best possible estimate of the hazards they face in order to plan for the future. If you are in a relationship with a cheater, you are living with a known hazard.

A problem with permitting risk to continue in your life is that risks are synergistic. Bad outcomes magnify and multiply like bad drug interactions. Add one risk to your life, like your husband is unfaithful, then many others come into play. He spends household money on the other woman, you are less focused on work and lose a promotion or pay raise, you take more sick days, your kids develop problems at school, you blow up at your mother-in-law, and you grow depressed. Contact with a hazard will change you, even if you don't understand how.

One woman who had an affair her husband didn't know about told us she noticed his behavior changed in the aftermath. He became distant and almost angry with her. He withdrew physically and emotionally. He started saying things like, "We got married for the wrong reason," and, "I haven't been happy for a while." Sometimes, on his way to work, he started crying for no reason. His conversations rambled. She wondered what was wrong with him, and when she asked what was wrong, he told her he was unhappy, he didn't know why, he was a bad communicator.

Then, one night, as they had a rare conversation about "us", he startled her with a question. "Back when you worked your other job, you got home late one night, about 11 p.m. When I asked you where you had been, you said the garage where your car was parked shut down with your car inside. I asked if you had your phone and you said, 'Yes.' Why didn't you call me?"

The woman told us she didn't remember the conversation and that's what she told her husband. But he persisted. "Were you 'talking' to someone back then?" She denied it. But he said again he felt for some time she was "talking to someone." When she asked him to elaborate, he became upset and didn't want to talk anymore.

"Could he know?" she wonders. "What do I do?"

Specialists in various fields refer to this type of scenario as "downstream effects." Lay people know it by another name: for want of a nail. For want of a nail the shoe was lost; for want of a shoe the horse was lost; for want of a horse the rider was lost; for want of a rider the battle was lost; for want of a battle the kingdom was lost. All for want of a horseshoe nail. A single negative event causes a cascade of negative events, and with cheating the damage ripples down to children, extended family, friends, job, and place in the community.

In a much-cited paper, Ali Siddiq Alhakami and Paul Slovic pointed out a peculiarity of risk.[7] People see a connection between risk and benefits even when it isn't there. For example, when we consider a course of action we want, we view it as having many benefits and a low risk. Thinking about actions we reject, we tend to view them as low benefit and high risk. In short, people typically see an inverse relationship between risk and benefit, even when the connection they see is an illusion. It's how our minds work.

This suggests if you want to stay in a relationship with a cheater for religious reasons, or because of loneliness, or because you are used to being mistreated, you will see the benefits of staying as high and the risks low. One man told us about a woman who went back to an unfaithful, emotionally abusive husband who previously abandoned her. When the estranged husband learned she was involved with another man, he cried, begged, and played the "I'm still your husband" card. He confessed to being the worst husband ever. He promised to do anything, including going to church with her. She took him back.

She explained her actions by saying, "Real love requires risk, putting one's feelings out there in the most vulnerable state. The thought of risking another chance with X [her abusive husband] scares me to death, but in reality, the risk would be no less with anyone. I believe this with all my heart."

Minimizing risk and magnifying possible benefits is what people commonly do when they decide on a course of action. It's also what some abused women do to justify staying with an abusive man, as in this case. This woman's claim that the benefits outweighed the risk was so preposterous all she could do was claim the risk would be the same with any other man.

We find the way risk is presented in books on infidelity to be unsatisfactory. In one book, for example, the authors admit the odds are against you rebuilding a stronger relationship after cheating. But they emphatically say, "Take a risk!" That risk is your life. Imagine a financial advisor giving you that advice about your lifesavings. It's like telling a teenager driving on two-lane country roads to pass cars on a curve.

Not only that, but saying a post-affair couple has a stronger relationship than before relies on self-reporting, and self-reporting is notoriously unreliable.[8] We believe what many authors on staying together are really dealing with is how people cope with the disappointment of unmet expectations. Two authors have characterized this process as "getting what you want by revising what you had."[9]

Specifically, people with unmet expectations do three things.[10] First, they forget the original standard, so they don't use it to compare with how they feel now. Second, they explain away failure by viewing the original standard as unattainable, instead of accepting that they failed to achieve it. Finally, people with unmet expectations compare themselves to someone who is worse off, even if that means inventing a hypothetical person or situation. So a woman might think, *At least he doesn't hit the children,* or a man might think, *At least she only cheated with one man.*

People apply whatever standard suits them to explain why they are staying. Often the standard they use is, *I'm staying, so I will claim things are better.* They may be staying for financial security, to prevent disruption in their social life, or so they don't have to get a job, but they will say something about the sanctity of marriage, trot out the trite "everyone deserves a second chance," or claim an improvement in their relationship. In short, people often won't tell you what their perceived benefit is, which is the real reason why they stay.

In addition to the problem of shifting standards of comparison, terms like a "stronger relationship" and a "good marriage" are ambiguous, and people's self-assessment of ambiguous terms is unreliable.[11] The final point to make is this. If there were no assessment of a relationship before cheating, there is no valid way to compare it to an assessment after cheating.

There are many risks in staying with a cheater. The first risk is you don't have a factual basis from which to make a decision. You simply don't know what happened, for how long, and with whom. The only person who can give you those answers has a strong reason not to tell the whole truth. The second risk is the other party will cheat again. You may wonder how they could possibly do this to you a second time. The answer is the same way they did it to you the first time.

In one study, psychologist Kayla Knopp and her colleagues followed 484 adults through two heterosexual romantic relationships.[12] They defined cheating as having a sexual relationship with someone not your current partner. They found that people who reported that they cheated in the first relationship were three times more likely to cheat on a subsequent partner.

That suggests there is some literal truth to the saying "once a cheater, always a cheater." But it goes deeper than that. After someone cheats on you, they will forever remain a cheater in your mind. That's the figurative meaning of the saying. Once someone cheats on you, you will not forget it.

When you weigh risks, there is another thing to think about. We are biased in favor of ourselves. We don't want to feel vulnerable. Research shows we are convinced that other people are more likely than us to suffer bad outcomes. Specifically, we believe others are more likely to experience skin cancer, a heart attack, tooth decay, a mugging, food poisoning, unwanted pregnancy, and an auto accident while on the phone than we are.[13] We are biased in favor of ourselves despite the odds.

Buy a lottery ticket every day for a week or every week for three months. You will quickly learn that not only do the laws of probability apply to you, they don't care about you.

As we turn off the cold shower of risk analysis, we leave you with a simple proposition. If you are thinking about staying with a cheater, the faster you analyze the risks the better off you will be. In addition, if you go to a professional for guidance, that professional has an obligation to thoroughly assess the risks and explain possible outcomes to you, including the worst outcomes. It is what the claim to professional knowledge means.

The problem with risk is that it does not smell.[14] Risk is like natural gas. It is odorless, colorless, and tasteless. That's why a chemical called mercaptan, which smells like rotten eggs, is added to natural gas. Unfortunately, there is no chemical that can be added to risk to make you understand the hazard. Though there are many books about getting past infidelity, we have not seen one that, in our judgment, provides a thorough, fact-based understanding of the risks.

The lesson from disgust, anger, suspicion, and trauma (DAST) is simple. To stay with a cheater, you have to defeat your own biology. The lesson from risk is also simple. You think you understand the risk? You don't. You think you're the exception to the rule? You're not.

It is disturbing to contemplate the risks involved in staying with someone who has betrayed you. That's why merchants don't forgive shoplifters, banks don't forgive embezzlers, and nations don't forgive traitors. They all understand the hazards of dealing with someone who cheats. We'll look at those hazards in more detail in our next chapter, the chapter on lying.

CHAPTER 8
LYING

"When we invent a story to mislead people, we try to figure out the story they want to hear, and we tell it."

—Roger Schank, cognitive scientist

Roger Schank, a pioneering researcher in computer intelligence, observed that human beings navigate routine situations as if reading from a script. In job interviews, for example, we arrive slightly ahead of time, looking our best, prepared to explain our work history and why we are dying to get the job. The interviewer follows her script, probing our qualifications and past performance. As Schank says, "Scripts are useful for understanding the actions of others as long as we know the script they are following."[1] But when we don't know the script, it's hard to act appropriately.

That was the problem facing Elizabeth Edwards on December 30, 2006.[2] Christmas, Elizabeth's favorite time of year, had just passed, and the holiday was even more poignant because she was in a fight for her life against breast cancer. With the holiday gone, Elizabeth's husband John, a former senator and serious contender for the presidency of the United States, approached her with a confession.

He had, he explained, been forced to replace his campaign videographer because he had a one-night stand with her. A single night, John reiterated, and he was filled with remorse. But, he added, there was no way to withdraw from the presidential race since he had recently completed a nationwide tour announcing his candidacy. To drop out would raise too many questions.

When she heard the news, Elizabeth screamed, cried and threw up in the bathroom. Two years later, writing about her husband's affair in her bestselling book *Resilience*, she would not deign to mention the other woman's name. This woman, she wrote, was "so completely unlike me" she was capable of standing "on a sidewalk in the hopes that some clumsy come-on line might work on a married man." Elizabeth agreed to let John's campaign go forward, though she knew she was sitting on information that could destroy his campaign and his party's chance of capturing the White House, if he were nominated. She knew thousands of people working on her husband's behalf might be wasting their time. But time was short, a decision had to be made, and the momentum of her life said, "Go on as before."

When Elizabeth Edwards made that decision, she didn't understand the cheater's script. She didn't understand her future was about to be determined by how things actually work, not by the screenplay in her head. Her hopes—what we would call the naïve victim script—led her to believe: *It's not too late to have my life back; it is the other woman's fault; I can accept what my husband says at face value.*

John Edwards' script, the cheater's script, said this: *Don't admit anything unless you have to; then say only the absolute minimum of what you must. Protect your own interests until you figure out what you want to do. Draw her into your plans. Express remorse. If possible, throw blame on her and the other party.*

The one-night-stand story John told Elizabeth, and which she presented in her book *Resilience*, seemed so implausible to us we were embarrassed for her. Not that Elizabeth wasn't intelligent. She was very bright. But she didn't understand what she was dealing with. As a political campaigner, she kept campaign staff up at night researching answers to questions. She said she mastered four times the facts she needed because she was determined to avoid the public humiliation of not knowing the right answer.

64

Yet, when John cheated, she was like a teenager at her first job interview. That is the classic problem for one with a cheater. They are so far behind the curve they are like a child trying to fathom the adult world.

Our discomfort watching her at the time, as she did nationwide television interviews with Oprah Winfrey and others, came because we saw her as the naïve victim who doesn't understand her situation. We had long understood both the naïve victim script and the cheater's script, and that made it painful to watch.

Elizabeth endured all the reactions we summarize as DAST. She felt disgust (she threw up), anger (John described her as "furious"), suspicion ("...even when he told the truth, he left most of the truth out"), and trauma (symptoms too numerous to mention). The emotional pain, Elizabeth said, threw her on the floor.

With so many secrets kept from her, she doubted she knew her own life story, and in the wake of neurological trauma, like most people, she coped in impaired ways. She overate. She tried to deny what happened. She said she sought to open a drawer and find her old life, but every time she opened it, she found her new life. She spent months trying to accept a single instance of infidelity and couldn't do it; then she discovered there was much more.

Eventually facts surfaced which refuted John's story. The one-night stand was a relationship, there was a sex tape of John Edwards and his affair partner Rielle Hunter, and despite John's public and private denials, he had fathered Hunter's daughter. An aide alleged that John promised Rielle Hunter, after Elizabeth was dead, he would marry her on a Manhattan rooftop with entertainment provided by the Dave Matthews Band.[3]

By the end of 2009, after another Christmas, Elizabeth Edwards realized she could no longer be John Edwards' wife. A year after *Resilience* was published, she added a final chapter in a revised edition. "One day," she wrote, "I did not want to try anymore." She "wanted to take a long shower and be away from the lies my husband had told me and the woman he told them about..." In January 2010, she legally separated from John. The following December, before she could complete her state's one-year mandatory separation prior to divorce, she died of cancer.

In time Elizabeth's story, like all our stories, will fade. In time it will be forgotten. But her story is timeless. It is archetypal. It is the naïve victim script pitted against the cheater's script.

A lie, moral philosopher Sissela Bok says, is a statement meant to make others believe what we ourselves do not believe.[4] We would define a lie this way: A lie is a false statement, intended to mislead, made by one person to a person who is entitled to hear and know the truth. In addition, the false statement injures or tends to injure the second person.[5]

Lies can be in the form of words, writing, action, or silence. A lie can be a gesture, a look, a nod of the head. Saying you are going to pick up the laundry when you are going to pick up the laundry and see your lover is a lie. The act of infidelity itself is a lie and betrayal.

Lies do not include politenesses like, "Your hair looks nice." Lies move beyond the realm of etiquette to the realm of ethics. Lies involve genuine harm to another. That's the essence of the lie; it is done knowingly and causes genuine harm.

Lies are traps for unsuspecting prey. One woman told us she and her husband bought a larger house with a larger mortgage, which required both their incomes. Only later did she discover her husband's long-running affair, an affair which began well before the purchase. Now, she writes, she is financially trapped in the marriage.

Another woman quit an extraordinary job to become a stay-at-home mom at her husband's urging. Two years later, she learned her husband encouraged her to quit because it made his affair easier to manage. Yet another example comes from one of our Direct Answers columns, a column we titled "False Memory."

Six months ago, right before our 27th wedding anniversary, I found out my husband fathered a child with a woman. The child is now 20. He confessed because I found receipts in his wallet that were child support payments made to the mother. I snooped because I knew he was hiding something, and I was desperate to find clues.

This affair happened during a difficult period. We'd been married seven years, and he lost his business. I remember thinking how distant he was, but my religion and faith made me always believe the best about him. Although I knew something was up, I never imagined he'd had an affair. I always chalked his behavior down to depression.

He and the woman signed some sort of agreement whereby he would help her financially but otherwise would remain anonymous. She kept it that way for years, but around 10 years ago, he says, she 'blackmailed' him into giving her more money. The receipts in his wallet were payments he made to keep her quiet and not tell me what happened.

He says now the situation made him "come to himself" and break off the relationship. They had only been together maybe three or four times when he broke it off, and a month later she told him of the pregnancy. I've met the girl, and there is no doubt my husband is the father!

In his eyes, he's been 'faithful' to me for 20 years. He took a lie detector test, and the results are he is telling the truth. I decided to stay married to him, but I'm struggling with trust. I wonder if he is the man I want to live with.

To his credit, he now seems to have changed many of his ways and attitudes toward the marriage. He is more concerned and attentive. He says he loves me deeply and wishes he had never done this thing. I know no one can read anyone else's mind, but do you have any advice for me?

-Julia

Julia, in Washington Irving's tale "Rip Van Winkle" a man catches a nap in the woods and wakes up 20 years later. At first surprised to think he slept an entire night, he is stunned when he returns home and realizes he slept through the entire American Revolution. The whole pattern of his memory is called into question.

Exactly like Rip Van Winkle, you have 20 years of catching up to do. Your husband is attentive now, but you suspect the change in his behavior is the difference between you knowing his secret and not knowing. Cheaters often get to stay until the one cheated on gets their mind totally around what happened.

What will dawn on you as time goes on? You will think about the time you wanted a trip and he said there wasn't enough money. You will think about the time you felt especially close to him and wonder if it was real. You will think about the time he said he didn't want another child and know the reason why.

He took all the options for himself and foreclosed all of yours. If you had known the truth then, you might have been married to someone else for the past 18 years. Give yourself time before you decide what to do. A cheater usually seeks immediate forgiveness, which they equate with a pardon. They want a pardon before their partner has a chance to think things over, a chance to catch up, and a chance to regain clarity. But like Rip Van Winkle, you need time to adjust your memory to what actually happened.

-Wayne & Tamara

People tend to believe others are telling the truth when they are not. If I had known the truth, I would have stayed on birth control, not tried to conceive, not quit my job, not bought the house, not allowed him to move me away from my family, not allowed him to tie up all our assets in his business. "If I had known then what I know now"—this is what the liar takes away from you.

A lie is an assumption of power over another. A lie is an assault that attacks not only the dignity of the other person but also their physical and mental well-being. A lie steals power from the one deceived. It reduces their alternatives. It causes the betrayed person to act as they never would have acted had they known the truth. A liar deliberately feeds inaccurate information, and when there are children, the lies reverberate in their lives as well.

As ethicist Sissela Bok says, "The greater the actual gap between role and reality, the more constant the need for concealment."[6] The more the concealment and the longer the concealment, the greater the damage. As we said in an earlier chapter, people tend to speak of betrayal as if it is one act, but even the simplest act of betrayal, the one-night stand, involves dozens of mental acts. A short affair involves hundreds, or, more likely, thousands of mental acts of deceit and duplicity.

Infidelity wounds because it is an attack from the human being with the highest level of access to our private, personal, intimate information. No one else possesses that kind of knowledge or that kind of power. In Shakespeare's play *Julius Caesar*, when Brutus refuses to share his plans with his wife Portia, she asks him a question. Within the bonds of marriage, she says, is my knowing secrets that pertain to you an exception to our vows? Then she adds, "Dwell I but in the suburbs of your good pleasure? If it be no more, Portia is Brutus' harlot, not his wife."

Last Friday night, I was caught with another woman by my girlfriend. When my long-time girlfriend came to my house, I told her I was going to bed early. She suspected something and came back to find this woman in my house. We had been cheating for about a year. The other woman didn't know either.

My girlfriend had a fit. She cursed me up and down and told me she wanted to hit me. After about 30 minutes of that, she left. On the way out, she keyed my car. Then the other lady had her say. Mostly she could not believe I would do this to her.

I felt as low as I could feel. I felt so bad for my girlfriend. It hurt me so bad. I finally realized she is what I was searching for in a woman. I need her in my life, but she may never speak to me again. She may never look at me again with those big eyes. That thought feels like a knife cutting me inside.

Why did I do it? I look back now and know it was because of ego and lust. I didn't go after the other lady. She came after me. I backed off several times, but she kept coming so I gave in. When that woman asked me several times if I was seeing someone, I said I had a friend but nothing heavy.

This was hard on me, very hard. I carried around a lot of guilt, which made me angry toward my girlfriend. My girlfriend knew something was up. She also kept telling me if I was interested in someone else to tell her. But I didn't want to lose her.

I told my pastor, and he prayed for us. He tried to call my girlfriend, but she would not answer the phone because she thinks it's me. Now my question is how do I get my girlfriend back?

-Tim

If we had to characterize this letter, we would call it an example of well-developed rationalizations used to generate plausible reasons to justify selfish behavior at the expense of others. That, of course, is the definition of a narcissist. Two of the lines that scream from the page are, "It hurt me so bad," and, "This was hard on me, very hard."

This robust element of narcissism is present in many cheaters. The young man who wrote the letter did something his religion told him not to do, but did he see his pastor then? No. He saw him after he got caught. He hopes to use his pastor as a Trojan horse to get his girlfriend back. In fact, he would still be cheating if his girlfriend hadn't caught him, and he blames the other woman, saying, "We had been cheating for about a year." But that woman wasn't cheating. For a year, she thought he was her boyfriend. When this young man sent us a second letter, his defensiveness, if anything, made it worse. He still regarded himself as a victim, not the architect of a grave injury to two women.

Cheaters give themselves a reason, a permission, for the affair. John Edwards first claimed he didn't know why it happened then later admitted he felt "entitled" to do it. The lies cheaters tell are often so juvenile or outlandish it's hard for an outsider to understand how they could be believed. But the person betrayed doesn't know the cheating script, and they are threatened with losing life as they know it—the life they hoped they would have. It is that life they try to cling to.

A woman told us while her husband was away on a business trip, she received a text message from a woman asking if she was happily married. When the wife asked how the other woman got her number, she replied at that very moment the caller was in a hotel room with her husband and he was taking a shower. Moments before, the wife had texted her husband, and the other woman could tell from the look on his face something was wrong. That's when she decided to wait until he was in the shower to check his phone.

Later, when the two women talked, the wife discovered this relationship had gone on for several years, and her husband told the other woman he was divorced.

When her husband returned home, she confronted him. He denied everything. He said he had been having dinner with a friend. Coincidently, all his text messages had been erased and he paid for dinner with cash, so there was no receipt. He explained the woman who called her was some psycho from his workplace who wanted to ruin his life. Though she had quit two years before, somehow she had been able to guess the two topics his wife texted him about that night: his activities at home and that they were trying to have a baby.

The wife wanted to believe her husband so badly she assured him everything was fine. A week later, she was troubled how this woman could have put two random topics together and why she kept his cell phone number for two years. When she investigated further, she found that her husband texted the other woman for two hours that day and they talked on the phone for 15 minutes.

When she confronted her husband, he had a simple explanation. The phone bill was wrong. A week later, she shoved the phone bill under his nose. This time he admitted he had talked to the other woman but over matters so insignificant he couldn't remember what they discussed. His alibi went further out the window when it became apparent a friend was lying to help him cover up.

Like many people, this woman said, "I don't believe in divorce," but since her husband wouldn't admit to cheating, she saw no point in counseling. She moved out and contacted a lawyer. Her husband won't confess, though he apologized for telling a few lies. She went on to say, "I feel terrible for accusing someone of something so terrible, especially a person I have been with for 10 years. As a result, I begin to wonder if he may be innocent..." But she knows the reason he won't tell the truth is that she would leave him if he admitted to cheating, plus he would lose face with his own family.

One of the problems with liars is they can cause you to doubt your own sanity. They deny so strongly you doubt yourself, even when what they say can't possibly be true. But if you go along with them, you are forever compromised.

It is not that liars don't value the truth. They do. What gives them power is that others are truthful while they are lying. Niccolò Machiavelli, the Renaissance political philosopher, wrote what could be the anthem for those who are unfaithful when he said, "...it has been a long time since I have said what I think or have believed what I said, and if I do speak the truth sometimes, I hide it among so many lies that it is difficult to find..."[7]

When cheaters lie, they force upon their victim something the injured party has not consented to. It exposes them to things like AIDS, gonorrhea, chlamydia, and genital herpes. It opens the family up to half-brothers and half-sisters. It takes resources of time, attention, and money away from the family. Sometimes it opens the victim up to being stalked or having the affair partner confront them at their place of work.

In subtle ways, a cheater's lies affect each interaction with the children. The child asks or needs something, and the person involved in an affair thinks about their plans with their lover and whether the child will interfere with those plans. At other times, the child senses a thing she or he can't define. But they know Mom's or Dad's attention is split between them and something else. In that way, the effects radiate further down the child's life, in ways that can no longer be traced.

Cheaters have a foot in two worlds, and one thing they rarely admit is they often don't regret their affair. As one man wrote us, "I told my wife of my emotional and physical infidelity and it almost killed her. Yet I felt no remorse or regret even though I should."

Another man confessed, "I can't get my affair out of my head, and I still don't regret it."

Bad as the effects of lying are, perhaps there is a way out. Perhaps there is a way of setting things right. That's what many people think when they turn to forgiveness, the topic of our next chapter.

CHAPTER 9
FORGIVENESS

"After such knowledge, what forgiveness?"

—T.S. Eliot, poet, playwright

I want to thank you guys for articulating what I have long felt about a marriage being forever denatured by an affair. Reading some of the websites promoting their affair-repairing services and reading 'affair-proofing' advice, I wondered why infidelity was such a deal breaker for me. Was I simply a less evolved, less forgiving type?

I know in my day-to-day existence I am not a grudge holder and have accepted many apologies from people and been fine. But I just could not put my finger on why I had no desire to reconcile after finding my two wives were cheaters. You articulate the reason very well, and it is something I felt but could not articulate: the desire to be loved to the exclusion of others and an aversion to having to remain ever vigilant in the future.

Thanks for putting forth this information as I know other betrayed spouses beat themselves up over the inability to reconcile. Your view makes so much sense to me.

-Ron

More from Ron will be found at the end of the chapter. You can flip there now if you like or keep reading as we explain more about how forgiveness and closure work in relationships.

We once read a scholarly book about forgiveness that contained articles from over 30 contributors. The most obvious lesson of the book is there is no general agreement on what forgiveness means. So, let us take the broadest definition of forgiveness we could find—the widest possible interpretation—and work backwards to establish what forgiveness should include and what it should not.

The definition we start with is one suggested by Robert Enright, a psychologist, and Richard Fitzgibbons, a psychiatrist. To forgive, they propose, means this:

"People, upon rationally determining that they have been unfairly treated, forgive when they willfully abandon resentment and related responses (to which they have a right), and endeavor to respond to the wrongdoer based on the principle of beneficence, which may include compassion, unconditional worth, generosity, and moral love (to which the wrongdoer, by nature of the hurtful act or acts, has no right)."[1]

Beneficence is an unusual word, not in most people's vocabulary. It refers to being kind or doing good acts, like shoveling snow off a neighbor's sidewalk. Another meaning of beneficence is a charitable act or gift.

We are intrigued by the Enright-Fitzgibbons definition of forgiveness. It says put what the offender is entitled to based on their actions, which is nothing, on top of what you are required to give them, which is nothing, and concludes you should offer the offender something—beneficence. A Venn diagram of the argument would show the victim and the offender as two circles with no point of intersection. Yet the authors claim there is something called forgiveness, which makes the circles overlap.

Enright and Fitzgibbons suggest this is a paradox, but it is not. A paradox is an apparent contradiction. This is an actual contradiction. Their 'forgiveness' applies only in a few limited situations, such as the attitude parents must take toward their children or the attitude all of us should take toward the trivial slights of everyday life. But as you move away from the parent-child relationship, as you move away from trivial examples and the overreactions of the oversensitive, the argument for farfetched forgiveness evaporates. If the Enright and Fitzgibbons definition of forgiveness is right, forgiveness is simply a rule that says people who do bad things always get to win.

There is no point in holding grudges or being irascible over small matters. For slights, no forgiveness is needed. Next day, things cool off and you let it go. Or they say, "Sorry," and it passes. Trivial things don't need forgiveness. But when we get to the serious matters of life, this idea of forgiveness breaks down.

"I gave as a victim, and now you are telling me to give again. That puts me in a way to be victimized a second time." That's what an injured person might say. If you raised a child like this, the child would never understand right from wrong. Even worse, others would always take advantage of her.

What has value is the first part of the Enright-Fitzgibbons definition. It is important to abandon resentment and bitterness because they undo you. They will ruin your life. Letting go of resentment makes hope, joy, and optimism possible; letting go resets your emotional counter to zero. Although it is difficult and may require time, freedom from bitterness is achievable. But to say the offended party must extend goodwill to the offender is more than ethically questionable. It is reckless.

In psychological terms, offering beneficence is a compensatory mechanism. It allows the victim to think, *I am the bigger person. I am the better person. I wish them well, so I win.* But the victim didn't win. They lost. Trying to perform the emotional contortion of beneficence locks the injured party into a struggle, trying over and over to feel good about a wrongdoer.

That reverses reality. It gives the wrongdoer a cookie for bad behavior and takes from the victim the only thing that says what the offender did was wrong. The victim is punished a second time. The Enright-Fitzgibbons definition, in its essence, contains the assumption that offering goodwill puts you on a higher spiritual level than the perpetrator. But you already were on a higher spiritual level, just as the honest man is above the thief. It assumes the perpetrator seeks redemption. But the world seldom works that way. When you offer beneficence to a perpetrator, they may not think you are beneficent. They may think you are stupid. It may make them more, not less, likely to take advantage of you in the future.

In a study by social psychologist James McNulty, newlywed spouses reported their spouse was more likely to show negative behavior after being forgiven than on days when they had not forgiven their partners.[2] Another of McNulty's studies, one tracking behavior over the first four years of marriage, found that more forgiving spouses experienced a constant level of psychological and physical aggression from their partner. Less forgiving spouses saw aggression from their partner decline over time.[3]

Reflecting this, some researchers refer to a forgiving attitude as "the doormat effect." As James McNulty speculates, when bad behavior is not met with negative consequences, it is in effect rewarded. When people receive negative consequences—like anger, criticism, rejection, and loneliness—they receive motivation not to reoffend.

The Enright-Fitzgibbons definition pushes forgiveness past sensible limits. You were seriously mistreated, but be a good sport about it. Wish the perpetrator well. Know your place, be dirt under the king's shoe, bake cookies for your rapist, learn how to care and feed the narcissist. Stomp on your own justified feelings to the benefit of the bad person. All that is contrary to our genes, contrary to our emotions, and it may be contrary to your sanity.

More than anything else, justice restores hope. When people affirm right over wrong, the result is a more moral world. It is a mistake to take away the revulsion and negative feelings we have toward those who commit grave crimes. When you tease out the implications of extreme forgiveness, it is impossible to defend as a moral act. It certainly contravenes justice, it certainly contravenes self-interest, and it may contravene the rights of third parties. Where is your obligation to warn and protect others from people who do bad things?

Amends, contrition, and compensation are what help one who has been injured. They show that the offender understood it, got it, and will never do it again. Still, as this letter shows, a problem remains.

My husband had two affairs last year. I am pretty confident he is not cheating now, and we are seeing a marriage counselor. He has changed much since I found out about what he was doing. He put our property in my name and bought me a $12,000 diamond ring.

He is affectionate most of the time. I believe this is proof that he loves me. The problem is I also have proof that he does not love me because he had affairs. So I have proof he loves me and proof he does not love me.

Our marriage counselor tells me his affairs are in the past, and I agree. The problem of the past is that one second later everything is in the past. To me, saying it is in the past is just a way to excuse anything. You could do almost anything and then later say it is in the past.

If you drive drunk and kill someone, can you say it's in the past? Just because you do not drive drunk anymore you can never bring that person back to life. It may be in the past, but it has certainly destroyed the future. That is the problem.

The therapist wants to focus on the present and future and consider the affair in the past. If this is a way to move on, then my husband can do almost anything to me and later be forgiven. He can even plan to do something and say to himself, "Later on it will be in the past."

Because something happened before and is not happening now is not a good reason to think it will not happen again. For me, because something happened in the past, it is more reasonable to believe it will happen again. After all, if he had not cheated, there would be no past cheating and no reason to say, "Put it in the past."

-Kayla

When you are victimized, you feel worthless. The one who is entitled to feelings of compassion, generosity, and unconditional worth is the injured party, not the one who cheated. What the Enright-Fitzgibbons definition implicitly admits is, "We can't stop you from being punched, so we will teach you how to take a punch." That is a philosophy for sheep. It is taking the gift we have for compassion and turning it against us. What does the wrongdoer need more than anything else? The understanding and restraint to stop doing wrong. They will not understand if there are no consequences.

Under too broad a definition of forgiveness, it is not the meek who will inherit the earth but the bad. We are not required to have positive feelings for the drunk driver who killed our parents or the man who raped our daughter. That turns the world upside down. Anyone with the stronger will gets what he wants. Offering rewards for behavior that does not warrant it shows no understanding. Even a normal person thinks, *If you give me a gift, you like me.*

When an injured party cannot make this farfetched idea of forgiveness work, they will beat themselves up again. It will be yet another thing they failed to achieve. The issue will become not the cheater's failure to stay faithful but "your failure to forgive". That is not the correct way to help someone who has been seriously injured.

By all means forgive, but know that forgiveness means giving up resentment and letting go of anger. That's it. Nothing in the nature of forgiveness requires you to keep the victimizer in your house or in your life. Nothing in the nature of forgiveness requires you to trust them again.

An idea closely related to forgiveness is closure. Closure and forgiveness come out of the same sack, and both are a search for a positive resolution to bad circumstances.

Closure is an idea with an interesting history in psychology. Originally it described the way our senses organize things. For example, think what happens when you write the letter K twice. First, write a K the normal way. Next to it, write a backwards K. Now push the two letters together. One might think we would see K and its mirror image, or see a W on top of an M, or simply see some lines.[4]

What happens, however, is that we see a diamond between parallel lines. That tendency of our mind to reorganize what the eye sees into certain patterns is what Gestalt psychologists originally meant by closure. The mind wants to see a complete whole.

This may be one reason why we get mad when our favorite television program is interrupted by a news bulletin. It may also be a reason why most people don't like literary fiction. Critics like to think the masses aren't sophisticated, but literary stories often end with a main character unable to solve the problem they had from the very beginning. That is inherently unsatisfying.

We often receive letters from people seeking closure. A relationship has ended, and they wonder why. *Why did he cheat on me? Why did she treat me badly? Why did he or she date someone else?* What many people don't realize is that relationships usually end with threads dangling in the air. That's the normal pattern. Most people never learn the true *why* behind another's actions. Everyone wants the imaginary 'closure', but the closure they want is to have what they want. That is why almost no one gets closure.

As a psychological concept, closure doesn't work. When a relationship ends, people don't want to learn why, they want to learn why not. *Why can't I still have what I want?* But if a man used a woman for sex, how will learning the truth give her closure? If a woman loved a man for his wallet, how can that truth give him closure? It is unrealistic to think that a person who used you will act contrary to their pattern. It doesn't matter how you got involved with them—whether you pursued them or they insinuated themselves into your life. Asking why traps you.

We cannot demand closure from others. They get to be who they are. When we demand closure, what we are really saying is, "I won't change. I want my answer. I want my prize." Closure, like forgiveness, does not happen between people. It happens within us. We say to ourselves, "This is done. It is finished. This is what was accomplished in the relationship; this is what could not be accomplished. Now I begin again." We get trapped waiting for, seeking, and demanding a closure that isn't going to happen. As long as we understand the trap, a failed relationship can't continue to imprison us.

Today, many people use the idea of closure to suggest a rewarding ending is always possible. But as sociologist Nancy Berns observes in her book *Closure*, a satisfying conclusion means different things to different people.[5] For some, closure might mean the end of a chapter, while for others it is a way to remember, a way to forget, a way to get even, a way to know, or a way to forgive. These six different meanings, Berns says, are illustrated by acts such as burying your father, raising a battle monument, burning old love letters, convicting a criminal, solving a mystery, or hearing a murderer confess.

No matter what ending people have in mind, Nancy Berns suggests, it always carries four assumptions.[6] Closure is possible, good, desired, and necessary. The problem with this view is that life goes on. It doesn't close. What people really need is a way to mend, return to wellness, heal, or end grief. The idea of closure, like the idea of forgiveness, promises but fails to deliver. We go on, we remember, we cannot change what happened. We try to stop rehearsing the drama in our mind because to rehearse it is to relive it and reduce our expectations for life in the here and now.

When we are traumatized, the goal is to reach the point where we live a full life. There is no escape clause called closure, or forgiveness, which says we get to bypass our emotions and memory. There is time, which can soften blows, there are new dreams and new hopes, and there are new courses to chart. But when it comes to cheating, our internal alarm system is always on. Once the alarm has detected a breach, it bays like a pack of beagles pursuing a fox.

Closure and forgiveness are both, in a sense, manufactured ideals. Life is a lot messier, and our emotions a complex mixture of grief, anger, sorrow, joy, and more. Trying to play Mother Teresa or Gandhi with a cheater will drive you nuts. Take them as ideals, if they inspire you, but don't think they found a bliss you must find. Don't let the search for forgiveness or closure make you batty. Letting go of anger and overcoming trauma symptoms is a big enough task. Move in that direction and closure and forgiveness will take care of themselves.

We began this chapter with a letter and conclude it with more thoughts from the same writer.

I think you two have it right on the natural response to infidelity being divorce. On some sites promoting their services, various experts claim that a high percentage of marriages survive and are stronger; the independent researchers, however, find that about 80% of relationships infected by cheating end. Marriages may survive at a higher rate than relationships, in general due to logistical and financial considerations. But, rather than getting stronger, as claimed, the majority limp along with lots of pain and resentment.

A friend from one site, a psychologist, contacted me after I was challenged pretty vigorously for suggesting a man with an unremorseful spouse might want to look at divorce as the best option. This friend is a practicing psychologist and deals with infidelity in her practice. She confirmed that most relationships do not survive and almost none are good after cheating. She also told me in her practice, the healthiest victims of infidelity she sees are those for whom it is a deal breaker. She said they heal faster and are more likely to have better second marriages.

So, thanks, again.
Ron

For reasons that he didn't consider at the time, Ron should have expected to be attacked by other people in that forum. We'll explain why in the next chapter. We will also explain why Peggy cried.

CHAPTER 10
WHY PEGGY CRIED

"We are free to make the wrong choice, but not to succeed with it."

—Ayn Rand, values theorist

The place was Washington, D.C. The event was a large conference on marriage. The topic was Preventing Affairs. The presenter was Peggy Vaughan.[1]

For 20 years, Peggy Vaughan had advised individuals whose spouse or significant other had cheated. She wrote books on the subject, and she spoke with the detachment of an expert. At the end of her address, she spoke about not wanting her three granddaughters to endure the pain of an affair. Then she "unexpectedly broke into tears."

Unexpectedly is Peggy's word, not ours, because what happened to her is commonplace. We often receive letters from people whose spouse cheated decades before, telling us they were once again caught off guard when their underlying feelings broke through. That is what happened to Peggy at the marriage conference. Earlier in her marriage, her husband James, a psychologist, cheated for seven years with 15 women. What is noteworthy is that James' cheating ended a quarter of a century before Peggy's public tears.

James Vaughan began cheating when he was a college professor.[2] Though he and Peggy had two children, James slyly arranged his in-town and away schedules so he could spend hours or nights with other women, lounging in bed with cheese, wine, music, and Manhattans. The one thing the women had in common was that they were much younger than James. During part of the time he cheated on Peggy, James conducted business seminars in which he preached the value of honesty and open communication.

Peggy said she stayed for two reasons. She didn't think she could make it alone, and she was too embarrassed to go home to her family. If there was a final reason she stayed, it was lifestyle. James was an exceptional earner, crisscrossing the United States on business, staying in first-class hotels and sometimes traveling to Europe or South America. The Vaughans lived in affluent communities like Hilton Head Island, South Carolina and La Jolla, California.

If her marriage ended, Peggy conceded, it would have to be James who pulled the plug. She would never make the decision to leave. Apparently, James stayed for the same reason a narcissist doesn't marry another narcissist, and he was candid about his reasons for cheating. He knew his wife wouldn't divorce him. "Why not?" was another of his explanations for adultery.

In 1980, James and Peggy Vaughan published *Beyond Affairs*, a book about James' affairs. The two of them promoted the book in a hundred interviews and on national television, and over the years Peggy became the public face of one who stays with a cheater. One of the eerie things about *Beyond Affairs* is the number of times James refers to his honesty, claiming, "I've never been a good liar."

He also claimed he was honest with his affair partners. To hear him tell it, none of the women thought they were in a relationship that might lead to marriage. As he said of one of them, "Our relationship was based almost totally on our mutual enjoyment of sex." Now, James had a Ph.D. in psychology and his master's degree was in clinical psychology. We cannot believe, as he suggests, all 15 women were so cavalier about intimacy. That is an impossibly naïve claim for a psychologist to make.

The woman he calls Terry, for example, kept coming in and out of his life, leaving in "sadness" and moving out of town when it became apparent she wasn't going to replace Peggy. With another woman, James admitted that accepting a job at a different university made it easier to give her the brush-off.

A decade after *Beyond Affairs,* Peggy wrote *The Monogamy Myth,* a book that excuses the cheater.[3] The trouble is Peggy's deeper self didn't buy it, and at the marriage conference her core revulsion with James' behavior reasserted itself. Injuries that heal are forgotten. Those that don't occupy our thoughts. What did her tears prove? This was not fixed, and she never got over it.

In the aftermath of her first book, Peggy began advising others with an unfaithful partner. Her informal counseling evolved into an organization, which she later turned over to Anne Bercht, a woman whose husband had sex with her almost nightly while conducting an affair with another woman. Bercht authored a book called *My Husband's Affair Became the Best Thing That Ever Happened to Me.*[4]

In many ways the flaw in the title is more interesting than the book. When people compose a list of the ten best things that ever happened to them, they list items like, "Saved for my retirement" and "Started an exercise program," not "My husband committed adultery and, as a result, my daughter tried (twice) to kill herself." While we can't live in the past and wish things never happened, we can't portray bad events as good things. It turns the world upside down.

What Anne Bercht's title calls to mind is a classic paper written by Ronnie Bulman and Camille Wortman.[5] Bulman and Wortman interviewed 29 people who were paralyzed in accidents, some from the waist down, others from the neck down. What Bulman and Wortman found is that most of these people found meaning in the accident by viewing it not as a misfortune but as something deserved or positive. Though these people were permanently crippled, most of them coped by adopting the belief that things turn out for the best. Many saw their accident as evidence of a deeper plan at work in the world, or as a part of a divine plan, and that is how Anne Bercht coped. As she wrote, "...it is clear to me that something supernatural was at work in my life at that time."[6]

This way of coping with tragic events has a name: the belief in a just world. Melvin Lerner, a sociologist, wrote a book about it. The book is called *The Belief in a Just World: A Fundamental Delusion*. As Lerner explained, no adult capable of tying his own shoelaces would admit to believing the world is really just.[7] There is simply too much evidence to the contrary. Yet research shows human beings often act as if they believe it is true. In psychological terms, the belief is helpful because it allows us to plan for the future and it quiets our fears.

The belief in a just world is easy to maintain when we see good people getting good results and bad people getting bad results. But it is challenged by the two opposite cases—good lives with bad results, and bad lives with good results. One ancient way to preserve the belief in a just world is the doctrine of karma. Karma explains apparent injustice by offering a view of the past, present, and future. Past lives determine the present, and present lives will determine the future.

Karma promises that our next life will be rewarded or punished by what we do with this life. Even though things seem temporarily unjust, karma says balance will be restored as beings move from one life to the next. Another ancient explanation for people getting more or less than they deserve in this life is the belief in heaven and hell. The good who suffer unjustly will be rewarded in heaven, while the bad will be punished in purgatory or hell. The result is the same as with karma. Justice triumphs.

Like the misdirection of magicians, many psychological experiments are built upon a lie. Researchers give people one reason for an experiment when they are interested in something else. Keeping subjects in the dark prevents them from consciously determining the outcome, and that is how research into the belief in a just world was conducted.

In one experiment, Melvin Lerner and his colleagues had a group of women observe two men, 'Tom' and 'Bill', perform a task.[8] The women were told the study was about individual contributions to a group effort. They were also told that for financial reasons only one of the men could be paid. Half the women were told Tom would be paid, while half the women thought Bill would be paid. In general, once the women learned who was paid, they judged that person performed better. But the research gets even better. In another experiment Lerner cites, students who received no reward tended to rate their own performance as inferior to students who received a reward, even though there was no difference in performance.[9]

In other experiments, observers were led to believe a research subject would receive electric shocks in a testing room.[10] Though no one was actually shocked, it appeared they were.

When observers were given the power to rescue or compensate the victim, they saw the victim in a neutral light. If they were not given the power to save the victim, most denigrated the victim. In fact, the worse the supposed suffering of the innocent victim, the lower the opinion the observers had of them. The observers wanted to believe the victim had it coming. As Lerner wrote, "Normal people will reject, or at least devalue, an innocent victim, if they are not able to intervene effectively to correct the injustice."

After the experiment was over, observers claimed the shocks really weren't that bad or the victims knew what they were getting into. That was wrong on both counts. Observers were told from the beginning that the shocks would be strong and painful, and they were informed victims were not forewarned the experiment involved electric shock.

The general conclusion Melvin Lerner drew is this. People believe rewards are deserved (even when they are not) and suffering is deserved (even when it is not). In addition, the less deserved the suffering, the more people blame the victim.

We often get letters from men and women who are innocent. When they describe their conduct, there is nothing we or they can find that they did wrong. Perhaps that is one of the reasons Elizabeth Edwards tried so hard to blame the other woman. She had no clue there was a problem in her marriage and no clue she was doing anything wrong.

A few years ago, a couple wrote us about their 27-year-old daughter. This young woman and her boyfriend had been together three years when he cheated with an ex-girlfriend. The daughter was devastated. Her parents wrote, "We saw her anger, her lack of self-confidence, her not eating, her depression, her second-guessing, her loss of faith (which had been her strength), and a total disregard for herself." Though the daughter lived in another state, the parents sent her to counseling and said, "It was heartbreaking to watch her go through all of this for over a year."

The parents wrote us again when their daughter renewed the relationship. The boyfriend, after spending a year with the other woman, left that woman when she cheated on him. Now he was back at their daughter's door, not due to genuine remorse but as "more of a reaction to his ex-girlfriend doing to him what he did to our daughter. He did not forgive his ex, and yet he asks to be forgiven."

Though friends of their daughter say he does not come across as her equal in education, job, manners, or maturity, they admit he is good-looking. Very often, when a woman clings to an inappropriate man, there is one thing about him that is the peg she hangs her hat on. In this case the peg was physical attractiveness. She can picture herself entering a room on his arm. That allowed her to ignore mistreatment. With another woman, the peg might be wit, an air of affluence and sophistication, or general intelligence.

Ultimately this young woman took her unfaithful boyfriend back. She told her parents, "I have tried, but no one else even looks at me twice."

Her mother told us this man is the first man her daughter slept with, and, as a result, she " ... has bonded in a way that should only have been in marriage."

Six months later, the mother wrote again. She said, "Frankly, I wish he would just go away, but since our daughter has forgiven his betrayal of sleeping with his ex-girlfriend, and now he has returned to our daughter after the ex-girlfriend slept with another...it sickens me. I really feel it's a sick relationship. Six years and they can't seem to say what the intent of the relationship is. They are still trying to figure it out."

People who stay in unhealthy relationships typically won't tell you the reason they stay, because if they did, you could take it away from them. They won't tell you because they don't want to listen to anything that disproves their faulty reasoning. They may stay because they are imitating a father role, a mother role, or the bond of parents who didn't belong together. That not only gets them into a bad relationship, it keeps them in a relationship that can't succeed. They may think, *It's too late to do better, I want to be married only once, I want my children to be with their father.* Or they may think, *I can't undo this, I still want the dream.*

They are like a man stopped for driving under the influence who thinks, *I can't get arrested for this.* The time to prevent that was before he got into his car. Though some couples stay together in the absence of reason, they are not a guide for the rest of us.

Trying to find reasons these couples stay together is like trying to find the reasons why a woman who has been hit marries the man. There is a reason, whether it is the way she was raised, recent abuse, or his good looks. Or she may think she can't get or doesn't deserve anyone better. Perhaps he was her first sex partner, or she has children by him, or he is playing father to her already existing kids. Perhaps she thinks she can't divorce because she will lose her religion. All those are reasons, she feels, worthy of staying.

But people don't abuse the guitar they love. They don't put their most prized possessions in the rain to be soaked. Abuse in the place of love points to a different reason for the continued connection.

At the end of the previous chapter, we promised to explain why Ron, whose letter we quoted, was attacked in an online forum for suggesting a man might divorce an unremorseful wife.

Imagine a group composed of people who have been cheated on. Some are married, some are in long-term relationships, and some are just dating. Who is likely to be found in the group? Obviously not those who have moved on. But the group will include those who just discovered their partner's cheating and wonder what to do.

The people most likely to stay in the group over time, however, share one attitude: "We were cheated on and we are not leaving the relationship." What holds them together? Boundaries. A group needs boundaries that separate those in the group from those outside, and they need continual reinforcement to keep on the path they have chosen.[11]

When Ron went looking for an online forum about cheating, he assumed he was in a forum that included a cross-section of people, a group open to all points of view. In reality, he was in a venue composed of those who, at least for the moment, thought they were going to stay with someone who betrayed them. The people who had moved on or were only casually involved with a cheater weren't there.

Who was there? People wanting to justify their path. People who wanted to discredit reasons to leave. The people who stayed in the group wanted to satisfy a need to belong, and they sought status by defending group ideals.

When Ron suggested the man might divorce his cheating wife, it threatened many members of the group. Ron moved himself from the ingroup to the outgroup. In a group composed mainly of stayers, he said, maybe that's not the right answer. Excluding people like Ron was one way the ingroup bolstered their feelings of belonging.

Why were some members of the group so vehement? Because they were so fearful. Suggesting their cheater might leave them put them in mind of things they didn't want to consider. "I don't want to get a job, I don't want my finances to change, I don't want to have to move, and I don't want my holidays to be different. I don't want to lose my friends or social circle. I don't want to be separated from people I like who work with him or her. I don't want to be a divorcee, a single mom, or a person without a partner. I don't want to diet and exercise and be on the dating market again. I don't want to admit I made a mistake. I don't want to hear, 'I told you so,' from my family or friends. I don't want to be changed in the eyes of my congregation. I don't want to be blamed. I don't want people saying, 'What did she do wrong?' I don't want to be judged. I don't want anyone to say, 'It's your fault.' I don't want the headaches, the hassles, or the uncertainties of having this happen. I don't want to be saddled with the kids. And, finally, this isn't what I planned."

Shared attitudes, feelings, and behavior hold a group together, not the personal qualities of the members. Research suggests that, over time, a group like this tends to become both more uniform in outlook and more extreme in defending that outlook. And that's what Ron ran into.

We began this chapter by asking why Peggy cried. The answer is Peggy Vaughan never felt her husband wanted her to the exclusion of other women. She turned being married to an adulterer into a career, and still she cried.

In this chapter, we brushed against two topics without calling them by name. The first topic is how people manage to stay, and the likely answer is through cognitive distortion. People often stay with a cheater by kidding themselves about their own and his or her motives. They also stay by trying to accommodate to the pain they feel and making it the new normal.

Those two topics, cognitive distortion and accommodation to pain, are the stock-in-trade of those people who tell victims how to stay with an unfaithful party. That's the group we call the adultery apologists. That group is the subject of the next chapter.

CHAPTER 11
ADULTERY APOLOGISTS

"...our therapeutic society seems to depend on an implicit as-
sumption that we are less likely to know ourselves than certain
licensed experts are likely to know us."
—William Ian Miller, professor of law

Go for a physical examination and a doctor will test your reflexes by tap-
ping your knee with a rubber hammer or shining a light in your eye. The
doctor wants to make sure your reflexes work the way they should.

Go to some therapists after your partner cheats, and the therapist may
act as if your body and mind are not acting as they should. That is not correct. Your body and mind are doing precisely what they were designed to
do. The most direct, unbiased, and truthful response to cheating you will
ever receive comes from your entire person the moment you learn someone cheated on you. It is a reflex, like the knee jerk, designed to protect
you. It is a direct perception of reality.

In this chapter, we will explore a few of the ways some people try to alter those direct perceptions. Most of the people we quote are therapists,
though what we say may apply to clergy, friends, and family.

Our comments are not personal. What we say is in the nature of a
brief book review of each author's published work, to the extent we can
gauge their meaning from words on a page. What we offer is an analysis of
the author's reasoning, and this chapter is included for a simple reason.
You can describe a thing in two ways. You can say what a thing is. That is

what we do in the previous chapters. You can say what a thing is not. That is what this chapter is about.

We call these people adultery apologists because in one way or another they appear to defend the actions of cheaters. The books mentioned are only a representative sample of ideas you may read about cheating. We suggest that, if you read these works, you don't read as if you are reading a novel. Novels require the suspension of disbelief, and you can't do that with this material.

Don-David Lusterman, a licensed psychologist, is the author of the book *Infidelity*.[1] When we read Lusterman's book, we were fascinated by the way actors, usually a cheater, are presented as the passive recipient of their own action. For example, about a married minister initiating a gay relationship, he writes, "He had a drink or two and found himself in the man's hotel room."[2] Of another man he says, "When he drifted into an affair at work, he was mildly surprised."[3]

In this book, it is almost as if affairs fall out of the sky like rain and land on the unsuspecting cheater. It is a rhetorical strategy that takes responsibility away from the actor. Describing one who acts as the passive recipient of the action is something no seasoned newspaper editor would tolerate from a cub reporter. It blurs rather than clarifies the event. Try reading a novel replacing every "he said" with "he found himself saying."

Early in his first chapter, Lusterman suggests that a person with a cheating partner might keep a journal to "try and figure out what signals you might have been missing..."[4] Apparently the problem isn't that your partner cheated but that you missed the signals. Naughty you. This reversal of roles grows deeper when Lusterman mentions a woman whose husband wouldn't come to therapy. "I suggested," he writes, "that, since Reggie would not come, it would be important for her to imagine that he was in the room, and even better if she could take his side, along with her own."[5]

96

That is a stunning statement, and it takes us back to the origins of the psychology of influence. As you may know, the Korean War (1950–1953) began when North Korea invaded South Korea. China and the Soviet Union backed North Korea, and the United States and other countries fought with the South. In the United States, a major scandal erupted when American servicemen, taken as prisoners of war by the Chinese, began collaborating with the enemy.

These Americans soldiers, trained to give only name, rank, and serial number, did much more. Many made anti-American statements, pro-Communist statements, or both. The disloyalty of the troops grabbed headlines in the U.S., enraged politicians, and embarrassed the military. The puzzle was how the Chinese got American prisoners of war to act in disloyal ways, ways not only disloyal to their country but disloyal to themselves.

That story is ably retold by Robert Cialdini, a social psychologist, in his book *Influence*.[6] As Cialdini explains, the Chinese knew to "start small and build." For example, to get a man to make statements against his own country, the Chinese interrogator might ask for agreement with a mild declaration, such as "The United States is not perfect." No matter how highly a man thought of his country, most men could agree with that. Later, the service member might be asked to list the ways the United States is not perfect. Still later, he might be asked to elaborate on his list by writing and sharing an essay on the flaws in the American system.

The process could be used in reverse, of course, by getting soldiers to admit positive things about China. Once they had said or written critical things about their own country, or complimentary things about their captors, they were trapped. They had committed themselves to a course of action, and, as social psychologist Cialdini points out, once a commitment is made, even a 'harmless' one, people seek to act in ways consistent with that commitment.

What fascinates us is how regularly compliance techniques like this are employed by the authors of books on staying together after an affair.

97

Often the innocent party is asked to admit to some imperfection as a person, which is a thing good people readily assent to. It is the nature of good, sincere people to believe they are not as good as they are or as they should be. In this way the subtle process of manipulating a blameless person begins.

By studying the Korean prisoner experience, as well as from a wide survey of the research on compliance tactics, Robert Cialdini reached one clear conclusion. People should "be very careful about agreeing to trivial requests."[7] In doing so, they are actively committing themselves to far more than they realize. Cialdini believes that compliance techniques change our self-image in a way so cunning we normally don't recognize what is happening. Having agreed to a small concession, such as, "I am not perfect," a person is open to having their entire self-image and history altered.

When we mentioned the story of the American prisoners to a psychiatrist friend, he confessed he hadn't heard it before. As we explained the sequence of admitting their country was not perfect, followed by writing a list, he listened intently. When we mentioned the next step was getting prisoners to write an essay, our psychiatrist friend blurted out, "And then you've got 'em!" Precisely. It didn't take long for this psychiatrist to understand what was going on, and that's what we thought when we read Lusterman's suggestion that a woman take her cheating husband's side.

The research on influence, persuasion, and compliance leads to one simple conclusion. When dealing with a cheating partner, take your own side and be very, very careful about what you agree to do, what you agree to write, and who you agree to meet. There are more compliance tactics than we have mentioned. In most of them, a person is asked to agree to a small request, which sets them on the path to making greater and greater concessions to their own disadvantage. It is the classic foot-in-the-door technique.

The next book we want to consider is *After the Affair* by Janis Abrahms Spring, a clinical psychologist. Spring opens her book with several judgments she says she does not make. Her first judgment is, "I don't make blanket judgments about whether affairs are, in themselves, good or bad."[8] Janis Spring maintains this stance is legitimate because an affair might be enhancing to one party even though it devastates the other.

What an intriguing idea. By that standard we shouldn't make blanket judgments about rape either because a rape may be 'enhancing' to one party while it devastates the other. The same is also true of theft. No accepted system of ethics or morality considers that view legitimate, and for good reason. If one-sided advantage is a satisfactory standard, then almost no behavior is wrong.

Spring's standard reminds us of a book by another therapist. That woman's book is called *When Good People Have Affairs*,[9] and it sounds like the first book in a series. If such a series existed, it might include titles like *When Good People Steal Your Life Savings* and *When Good People Have Sex with Your Child*. What the title attempts to do is give the social benefit of acting with integrity to those who act without integrity. The title blurs and even denies a sense of right and wrong, and that is the same error with Janis Abrahms Spring's first judgment.

Life has direction, and that direction is the basis of right and wrong. If you think life does not have direction, if you think there aren't clear rights and wrongs, spend time with those raised in emotional abuse, in physical abuse, or in neglect. Spend time with those raised by alcoholics, drugs addicts, or career criminals. These people are damaged because they were subjected to conditions that violate the direction of life and tipped them into illness and dysfunction.

Janice Spring's second judgment is, "I don't separate the two of you into victim and victimizer, betrayed or betrayer." She explains by saying, "Each of you must accept an appropriate share of responsibility for what went wrong."[10] There are multiple problems with this statement. First, as one anonymous online reviewer pointed out, the notion that the betrayed party contributed to the affair is probably not even a testable idea. What Spring's second judgment does is to pre-decide the victim is blameworthy, an assumption which is biased and, as far as we can tell, without foundation in research.

When Spring says she doesn't separate the two parties into victim and victimizer, or betrayed and betrayer, it is as if she doesn't understand the criteria for betrayal or victimization. To the party injured by the affair, Spring says, "You may have a hard time admitting complicity..."[11] Of course you would.

In Chapter 5 we mentioned that victims of serious trauma often blame themselves for what happened, even though they are blameless. We don't know how Janis Abrahms Spring applies this statement to the people she treats, but what we will say is this. If any therapist uses this known fact about trauma to suggest you share blame for an affair, they need to prove to you and to their colleagues in the field of trauma recovery why their approach is ethical or supported by research. Our suggestion is, if your therapist suggests you are responsible for a partner's affair, get up and leave.

There are other things we could say about Spring's way of reasoning, but we will add just one more. She claims, "Regardless of your choice of partners...you're going to have to work hard to keep your relationship alive and well. If you think otherwise, you're still deluding yourself."[12] In making this claim, she is like the oncologist who has forgotten there are people without cancer.

We have two objections to her assertion. First, it isn't true. Well-married people don't 'work' on their relationship. Life may be work, often hard work, but a good relationship is not. Both parties feel the difficulties they face come from the challenges of life, not from the one they married. In fact, if your relationship is hard work, it is an important sign you are with the wrong person.

Second, the notion that all relationships are hard work is chilling. Consider the quote we gave earlier from a woman who returned to her abuser: "The thought of risking another chance with X [her abusive husband] scares me to death, but in reality, the risk would be no less with anyone." That woman equated the risk of staying with an abusive husband to the risk of staying with any other man. That is ludicrous, but it echoes the logic of those who maintain all relationships are hard work.

Claiming all relationships are hard work comes with the implication that if you don't do the hard work, you are a shirker. That is not representative of your situation. It also implies that if you do the hard work, you will receive a reward because the outcome is under your control. That's the just world idea, which Melvin Lerner called "a fundamental delusion."

That brings us to Esther Perel's *The State of Affairs*. The central fact of this book, and its biggest understatement, is found in her introduction. Perel says, "Mine is not an evidence-based scientific survey..."[13] We agree. But when someone eschews evidence and science in their introduction, it doesn't invite less scrutiny to their reasoning. It invites more. *The State of Affairs* is not based on empirical evidence interpreted in accordance with scientific method. Instead, the author takes a brief quote from someone and acts as if it constitutes evidence.

The State of Affairs is anecdotal, impressionistic, and autobiographical. What it lacks in logical structure it makes up for in purple prose. Perel mocks people in her office as "consumers of the modern ideology of marriage."[14] She calls monogamy "the sacred cow of the romantic ideal."[15] And she asserts that, "The human imagination has conjured up a new Olympus that love will remain unconditional...for the long haul with one person."[16]

Perel questions "the assumption that unfaithfulness is the mother of all betrayals."[17] Of course, calling it the mother of all betrayals is a straw man. She sets up an imaginary argument so she can knock it down. She's about to claim that other things are worse than cheating so the reader should be less sympathetic to victims of cheating.

As evidence, she offers Dexter (who bullies his wife), Julie's husband (a workaholic), and Russ (addicted to crystal meth). Then she asks, "Why is one form of diverted attention an indisputable violation of trust, while another gets couched in nicer words?"[18]

The specious argument she uses is equivocation. It's the fallacy of calling different things by the same name. She groups domestic abuse, work addiction, and chemical dependency as if they are equally forms of betrayal along with cheating. But no one discusses those things as betrayal.

If we wanted to find equivalents to the act of betrayal in cheating, we would use examples like these: a trusted family member molests your child, a physician orders a surgery for her own financial gain, or a man betrays his country. But domestic abuse, work addiction, and chemical dependency are not acts of betrayal, and the other person involved has continuous knowledge of what is going on.

Esther Perel attempts to weaken the concept of betrayal in another way when she discusses jealousy. People in Anglo-Saxon cultures, she claims, talk about cheating in terms of "betrayal, violated trust, and lying." The real problem, she says, is jealousy. The victim of the cheater is not acting out of a sense of betrayal, they are simply jealous. According to her, the victims deny their jealousy because they want to feel superior to the cheater. Perel claims, "Jealousy is denied in order to protect the victim's moral superiority."[19]

Saying the victim of the betrayer is simply jealous is yet another way to denigrate the person betrayed and the pain they suffer. Jealousy is always seen as a negative, and her statement is the argument a hardcore cheater would make. It is simply stunning to hear a therapist make the same argument. "Look, you're just jealous. All these women (or men) want to have sex with me. No one wants to have sex with you." That is the implied core of her argument.

In the final few pages of her book, Perel describes three categories of couples who stay together after an affair.[20] She calls them sufferers, builders, and explorers. Sufferers stay despite being miserable. Builders try to go on as before. Explorers, her highest category, want "to find ways to collaborate in transgression." Explorers have "chosen not to ignore the lure of the forbidden, but rather to subvert its power by inviting it in."

She explains that some explorers might have a date night at home after the babies are put to bed. Other explorers invite transgression by going to sex parties and speaking only French, by deliberately flirting with other people, or by searching online for others to join them in threesomes. Let's ignore the first behavior—date night at home—because it has nothing to do with the other three. Date night at home is a staple of relationship books, and it is something builders and perhaps even sufferers might do.

Let's focus instead on the last three behaviors. Esther Perel lionizes the tart and the tease. Her explorers try to elicit a sexual response from other people for their own amusement and pleasure. What Perel fails to mention is that flirts and swingers are chronic mischief-makers in the relationships of others. Because they don't recognize the boundaries of exclusive relationships, they can't be trusted.

Perel defines trust, not as an assured reliance on the truth or character of another but as an engagement with the unpredictable. That is not what trust is. That is what life is. And the central question hanging over *The State of Affairs* is why Perel redefines terms like jealousy, courage, and trust to make arguments a cheater would make.[21] A reader might wonder, *What does a person do when their therapist has them on the ropes while raising the cheater's hand in the air?*

Esther Perel's *The State of Affairs* is an example of motivated reasoning, which attempts to prove a predetermined conclusion instead of following where the facts lead. When *The New Yorker* posted its review of her book online, it headlined the review with: IN DEFENSE OF ADULTERERS.[22]

In general, books on infidelity try to spruce up and polish the image of the cheater. Though they give a nod to the pain of the victim of betrayal, they tend to be the cheater's best friend. If we summarized our objections to the adultery apologists under one heading, it would be this. They are making back-door public policy, and it is a public policy that works to the disadvantage of honest people.

The anthropologist Pascal Boyer suggests looking at cheating under two aspects.[23] First consider when cheating is a high-risk, low-benefit strategy; then consider cheating when it is a low-risk, high-benefit strategy. To demonstrate, Boyer uses the example of line jumping. When we allow people to cut in front of us in line and do nothing, we make line jumping a low-risk, high-benefit strategy. It creates more line jumpers. For that reason, Boyer explains, most people feel anger when line jumping occurs, even when the line jumper is in another line that does not directly affect them.

Honesty only pays off when we are prepared to punish cheaters and when we are outraged cheating isn't punished, even if we bear no cost. The existence of people who tolerate cheating is a threat to our own safety because it makes cheating a viable strategy. We may receive a loss from the cheater at a later date. That's why cheating must be exposed and found unacceptable.

Unfortunately, the general tendency of the adultery apologists is to make cheating a high-benefit, low-risk strategy. Adultery apologists imply there is no definitive word on the issue, but there is. Our view is that staying with a cheater is something you might do, but you will pay a heavy price.

Now and then, we receive an email like this:

I need urgent help. I cheated on my wife. The only thing is I told the woman I cheated with I was going to confess to my wife. The other woman then took it upon herself to tell my wife, but she lied. She said I hit on her and she turned me down. I kept the secret too long, and it backfired on me. Now my wife knows. I'm waiting for her to get home. Please help me. She gets off at 3:30 p.m. It's now 3. I just found your website. I have 30 minutes. I don't know what to say to her.

-Eric

In the shadow of that panic-stricken letter lurk two figures: the other woman and the other man. Who are they? They are the topic of our next chapter.

CHAPTER 12
THE OTHER WOMAN (OR MAN)

"The truth may redden your eyes, but it won't blind you."
—Ahmadou Kourouma, novelist

Wayne and Tamara, I read some of your online advice and liked your direct-
ness. What do you have to say to me?

So began a letter from a youngish businesswoman in an Asian city. She labels herself "the other woman." She is twelve years younger than the married man she's having an affair with and the affair is new, only six weeks old. She met the man by chance through a mutual friend, and she says she never married because she values her independence and is a bit selfish.

She's been in Asia three years; her lover is a new arrival. In four months his wife and two teenage daughters will join him, and the entire family will make this city their home for at least two years. The letter writer, Poppy, is "even preparing for the arrival of his family." She admits this is crazy given the "seeming dead-end inevitability" of the relationship. Of their marriage, Poppy says,

They seem in many ways to have a good marriage, not perfect, but very
whole with good children, open discussions, and lots of love. Except for me,
everything is good.
I've left him once quite dramatically when he was in the shower. But I re-
turned because I love him, and because he asked me to...we share a

(hypocritical) desire to be honest, passionate, and sensitive. We discuss work and love and spirituality, and we exercise and cook together. If we weren't having a steamy sexual affair, we'd just be very good friends that his family would have to accept... We spend time with colleagues from his work, one of which definitely knows we are having an affair.

There is an elegant craziness to her letter, an is-he-the-one breathlessness in what she says, mixed with the knowledge that she is speeding down a cul-de-sac. She wants his wife to "know he loves me and we were together," and at the same time, she doesn't want his wife to know. Yet she is sure the wife will "intuit" what happened, and she rationalizes that his relationship with his wife "may well grow positively because of it."

Poppy claims "this affair should not be vilified in any way in the adult world," and in the very next breath mentions her worry that his daughters will find out and lose respect for their dad. To kill their respect and admiration, she says, would be "a true crime." She also admits the affair stops her from forming stronger ties with friends and men who aren't married, and it weakens the ties she has to friends and family in her home country.

Perhaps this will all just die out as the day of his family arriving looms near, the memory of which will fade with the laughter of his girls and the reassuring presence of his wife and the life she will set up for them: the dinners, the wine soirees with colleagues, the richness of their new life in Asia. I can see it happening no other way in fact... and so the greatest illusion belongs to me, in not being able to fully grasp what is and what isn't.

Though the affair deprives Poppy of sleep and puts a strain on her work, she can't stop returning for one more dinner with him, one more conversation, and one more Sunday. In the most intriguing line in the letter, she writes, "We have consecrated his new family apartment together."

For a few women, an affair is power or a way to achieve power, more like a man. They trade sexuality for advancement, not necessarily at work but to have all the hounds sniffing after them and to show their dominance over other women. For these women it is: "I don't care about the wife; I don't care about the kids; I'll burn the house down to get what I want, even if it doesn't last."

Poppy left her mark in the wife's new home and in the wife's new bed. She takes satisfaction in thinking the wife will one day see her husband's smile on the other side of the bed without realizing it is his lingering memory of Poppy.

A man writes:

I have been involved with a married woman for six months. I know her husband through an organization he runs, and I began speaking to his wife online. She is very outgoing, and we began instant messaging. Most of the talks were friendly and comical, and I told her I liked her. Eventually we met and, upon being alone, ended up making out. Neither of us can be blamed for what happened because we both kind of pushed the issue. I am a very realistic person, and I'm guessing she doesn't love me like I love her.

With her husband, she has two children. I know she's not stupid enough to diminish her self-interest because her situation now is far better than it would be with me. I'm looking into justification for my next action. I love her. I know she doesn't want to be caught, and I'm wondering if it's best to walk away or to increase the chances she will be caught.

-Martin

There is a malevolent selfishness in Martin's letter, but some people in affairs are less calculating. A Canadian woman writes:

A few years ago, I suffered several traumas within the space of a year. My father died, and my mother, out of grief, attempted suicide. The town I live in was hit by severe economic problems, problems so severe most of my friends moved away.

I went through a period of extreme neediness without many people around me. The people who were around me, by the way, were also reeling from the loss of many friends. I made an effort to meet new people, but, unfortunately, most of the people who stayed are 15 or 20 years older than me.

The only reason I stayed was because I held a good government job, a job I trained many years for and one I was lucky to get. The year all this tumult occurred, I was given a permanent position. I was torn. Personally I was shattered, while professionally I was flourishing.

The last four years have been extremely difficult. The loneliness was unbearable at times, so I took solace in the bottle. I became so concerned about it last spring I called my mom to come and get me. I took leave from work and returned to my hometown. Being around my family and old friends made my desire to seek oblivion disappear. But when I returned here, I again found the loneliness overwhelming. I met a married man, and, because he was so kind to me, began an affair.

This is the first time I have done anything like this. My ethics have always led me to act with integrity. It's madness, I know, but the pleasure, however stolen, that I get from this man is intense. I'm sure it's driven by loneliness and fantasy. I don't have anyone to confide in, so I guess I'm not asking for advice, just support. I know what I have to do, but I'm scared to be alone again. I'm scared to leave a job I love and return home to look for work.

-Tess

Tess explains her motivation clearly, but what is the motive of the married man she cheats with?

Researchers Melissa McTernan, Patrick Love, and David Rettinger found that romantic cheating is typically associated with the personality traits of sensation-seeking and impulsivity.[1] Impulsivity refers to choosing the immediate over the long-term, and sensation-seeking refers to a desire for the novel, the intense, and the risky. These researchers found that, of the two traits, sensation-seeking was the more powerful motivation. Their study suggested that, "Individuals poor at perspective taking will also be more likely to cheat on romantic partners." In other words, cheaters look at things from their own point of view, not the point of view of the one they injure.

In addition, the researchers speculate, "It is also possible that relationship cheaters assume no harm will accrue to their partner because the partner will not find out about the transgression." However, they note, "The harm that comes as the result of the transgression is not solely the result of their [the victim's] knowledge of the transgression. There is an objective harm to being cheated, either in a relationship or in a social contract, whether the victim is aware or not."

Another harm to the victim is the loss of trust that forces the victim to live in the halfway state of knowing and not knowing. A woman told us,

I discovered my husband was involved with a former coworker four years ago… He said he didn't want the marriage to end, but I made it clear in order for us to survive, she had to be totally out of the picture.

Well, I caught him communicating since the discovery and even caught him at her house one early morning, thanks to the use of a GPS tracking device. I strongly suspect he is involved with her again. I am finally ready to throw in the towel but do not want to until I have positive proof. He will never admit it. Should I try to fix it yet again or resort to some sort of spy device to confirm my suspicions?

This writer, like some others, clings to the idea she must catch her partner red-handed in order to part from him. The expression "red-handed" refers to an ancient legal principle. The idea was that a person who butchers a stolen animal can't be prosecuted unless they are caught with the animal's blood still on their hands. Some victims of cheating cling to the idea of red-handedness to avoid facing reality.

Some letters we receive are simply from two people who should never have married or, more precisely, one person who knew they should not say, "I do."

I am a 32-year-old male, married for five years. My marriage life has not been a happy one, mainly because I seem to daily regret having married the woman I married. Even as I said my vows, I knew I was not totally honest—and somehow, as stupid and ill-judged as it sounds, I went through with it. Perhaps as a consequence, I have never felt really committed to her as a wife and have cheated on her throughout our marriage.

The reason for not wanting to marry her in the first place was that I felt our values and loves are vastly different. As such, I think we are unable to be fulfilling to each other, and I often think that we are merely meeting a social expectation by remaining married. Now I feel I need to move on and find real happiness for myself, but I have no idea how to end the present marriage.

We have no kids, so it should sound easier, but I honestly don't know what to do. I have been to a counselor, but I ended up having an affair with her. Would you have any advice for me? This is a crisis in my mind, heart, and life.

-Jacques

A woman in a similar situation writes:

I'm 25, married for six months. There are two issues for me: one, I got married for the wrong reasons to the wrong man, and two, I am currently sleeping with my 40-something married coach.

The first of my problems is that in the three years since my husband and I got engaged, we've taken different paths and grown far apart. I became active and started eating healthy, while he stayed sedentary, eating hot dogs and cookies all the time. I am a triathlete and travel the country competing. I eat an athlete's diet, organic and natural only.

I do this for health and because of beliefs I've developed about farming and the environment. My husband doesn't even have a gym membership and refuses to eat healthy. This is the way he's always been, but until recently I guess I ignored how much it bothers me. I made the mistake of thinking he would change, especially after we married.

I make a conscious effort to show interest in things he does, but I can't talk to him about my training because he doesn't listen. He never comes to my races. It is hurtful because I work so hard and love what I do. I feel we no longer have enough in common to have more than a basic friendship.

The second issue is my coach. He approached me at the gym a few months ago, asked if I had a coach, and asked if I wanted to be part of his team. I joined his team and at first we had a normal coach-athlete relationship. Then it escalated to a sexual level after he emailed one day saying I was beautiful and had pretty eyes.

He is married with two children. When it started, we agreed it would be physical only because we didn't want our spouses finding out. I have no problem with that, but he seems to push the emotional side of it. He calls me when he is out of town. He emails from work all day, and we go back and forth about sex, training, and relationships.

He will ask, "Do you miss me?" Or say, "I felt a spark last night at the pool." Or he will mention, "You are definitely someone I could fall for." Then he will turn around and say if it gets emotional it has to stop. I know this all makes me morally bankrupt and a huge cheater, but I've gotten myself into it and don't know what to do.

-Sally

Sometimes the "other woman" or "other man" is completely in the dark. Remember the young man in Chapter 8 who was cheating on two women? Neither woman knew about the other and neither woman was cheating. They simply fell for a lie they were told. A big problem for the partner of a cheater is that they don't know what the other person knew or was told. The other woman or other man could be as innocent and in the dark as they are.

But even if the other woman or man knew what they were getting into, they made no promises to you. Your partner made promises to you, no one else.

Often a cheater excuses what they did as just sex or as a mistake. That isn't true. A mistake is knocking over a glass of milk with your elbow. Cheating is an intentional act. Saying it was just sex is like saying the creature they had sex with is an inanimate object. But every time people have sex, emotion, attachments, and history are involved. The only time you can have "just sex" is when you are alone.

We close this chapter with a letter that poses an intriguing question. It is from an "other woman" who… Well, let's simply let her speak.

I've recently had an experience with a serial adulterer. I was one of the 'collection.' Learning and watching how he was living such a secret life was and still is amazing to me. He set it up so he would have the pick of his 'collection' right from his workplace. The women in the 'collection' never knew about each other because they were protecting him, a married man. It was a secret.

I became his work friend, through work and someone who was my work friend. She confided in me that she had become his lover. I suspected something but ignored my instincts. After all, he's married. He always ends these affairs by saying he's not sure what he wants.

After he ended it with her, even though I knew about it, I became one of the collection. Then I felt like a fool, and now I feel like I am armed with the new knowledge and power to make a huge difference. But first, I forgave myself for such a terrible lapse in judgment and horrible mistake I will never make again.

I watched and observed as he chose his next one for his collection, (how? we work in the same place), and then the one after that, and yes, the one after that. He continues to live this lie, claiming the usual, that it is his wife. While never really attacking her, he states they never have sex and they can't talk about things.

It took me quite some time to realize this person's character is seriously flawed. I know we are all human, tough times can happen in a marriage, and affairs happen. People do overcome them and stay married. This is so different. It's particularly intriguing because most of his male friends know of his behavior while the women do not. It appears he also participates in this union of his male friends who have that double standard and how they devalue and disrespect women.

I came to the conclusion what he is doing to his wife is without any doubt the same as physical abuse. We seem to turn a blind eye to knowing that a fellow human being is being psychologically abused, and emotionally, and forever damaged by this type of betrayal. There was a time when, if a woman or even a child was being physically abused in the home, it was "family business, and stay out of it."

These days it is a criminal offence. To me, he is kicking and punching and stabbing his wife in the heart repeatedly, without her even knowing. Until now. I was agonizing whether I should bow out gracefully, thinking that maybe it's none of my business. Really, it's between him and his wife. I've evolved from that. If I knew he was beating her, I'd intervene one way or another. So I've intervened, I've called her to tell her. And I've written a letter to her as well.

One of the realizations I came to when writing the letter is the tangents of damage and pain that have been caused by his behavior have become serious reverberating ripples throughout all of our lives and have, without question, left permanent scars on our souls. I had to tell her. My final thought is: When do we stop turning a blind eye to the emotional abuse this serial adultery causes? When will it become just as unacceptable as physical abuse has become in our culture?

-Elise

Was Elise right to tell the wife? Good question. It's the question for our next chapter.

CHAPTER 13
SHOULD I TELL?

"For every good reason there is to lie, there is a better reason to tell the truth."

—Bo Bennett, writer

We are going to explain our position on the "Should I tell?" question through a series of past newspaper columns. Rather than giving you the principle we follow, we will give the circumstances from which the principle arises. In each answer we could have said more, but, as always, we were constrained by the limits of print newspaper space.

We will start with a difficult case:

Old Sayings

I was recently involved in an eight-month affair with a married man. My affair with him was not his first. When ending our affair, I swore to him I would not betray him to his family since I take responsibility for knowing what I was doing when I got involved with a married man.

Although my decision not to betray him to his wife and family remains unwavering, I would like your opinion in reference to his wife. Should she know she has been deceived? I think if the tables were turned and I was the one being cheated on, I would rather know.

-Lauren

Lauren, your decision not to betray him to his wife and family may be unwavering, but the truth is you would like to tell and make him pay. Revenge is a powerful motivator.

A myriad of sayings apply to the three sides of this triangle. Four that come to mind are: confession is good for the soul, there is no honor among thieves, what goes around comes around, and knowledge is power.

Why should your promise to him mean more than his vow to his wife? Why should the word of a woman willing to cheat be good?

We are in a quandary. Should we support you in telling when your motivation is nothing more than revenge? Or should we consider the wife's vulnerable position, not knowing her husband is having sex with multiple partners?

Almost always we answer the letter writer, not other involved parties. We cannot protect this married man because his position is the least defensible. Being involved with other women is a betrayal to his wife every single time. But his wife, the person most in need of this information, did not write us. And what about you? Will you learn anything or change if you tell?

Mark Twain said, "Therein lies the defect of revenge: it's all in the anticipation." Revenge is cold comfort. It doesn't advance your life. That is one thing you could learn. Francis Bacon said, "A man that studieth revenge keeps his wounds green." That is another thing you could learn but may not.

From among all these sayings, which one do we believe is most important? Knowledge is power. Someone here could benefit from the information you possess. His wife. Go ahead and tell.

-Wayne & Tamara

After publishing that column, we received the letter below.

I read a letter and reply in your column "Old Sayings." The writer, Lauren, was considering telling the wife of a man she had an affair with about his extramarital activities. You encouraged her to tell.

I am baffled. You encourage a woman who is equally guilty to go and possibly ruin a marriage. Tell me something. What happens if this married couple has kids, how will it affect them? Do you know anything about the wife? Maybe she is the root of the reason why this man seeks other women.

So why encourage heartache and certain trauma? I have an old saying for you as well: what you don't know can't hurt you. Quite fitting for the occasion don't you think?

-Gregory

Gregory, we didn't receive a single letter from an innocent party who wouldn't want to know if their spouse was unfaithful. People who deal with reality seek to know when they are at risk so they can protect themselves from AIDS, herpes, paternity suits, and the other consequences of betrayal.

A rock climber takes the risk of falling. A cheater takes the risk of being caught. Rocks can't tell, but a spurned woman can. You suggest ignorance is bliss, but it is not. It is ignorance. What if the lump is malignant? You ignore the lump at your peril.

Not telling is not an option with a serial adulterer. Telling won't ruin the marriage, cheating will.

-Wayne & Tamara

Our cardinal principle is everyone being cheated on has a right to know they are being harmed. That is the only thing that puts control in the hands of the innocent party. Cheating occurs in the safest of places, our home. We weren't attacked in a dark alley but in our own home.

Someone who takes up rock climbing or BASE jumping accepts a level of risk. The one who undertook the risk is the one who bears the risk. Why does a cheater say cheating is a private matter and not the business of outsiders? Because it is to their benefit. But people who know get to do what they will with that information. The cheater doesn't own those people. The cheater doesn't get to decide what others can or cannot do.

Cheating stopped being a private matter when a third party entered the relationship.

The cheater's position is, "Don't tell." That makes those who know either an accomplice or an accessory after the fact. Our answer is "Tell," even if you need to do it anonymously.

A woman writes:

Dishonorable Discharge

Seven years ago, I was involved with a married military officer. In the beginning I was unaware he was married. He chose to tell me after three weeks. After a lot of back and forth and pursuing me, I weakened, and the affair lasted six months. Then he, his wife, and children were moved to another duty station.

In the ensuing 18 months he came back for training and each time would contact me. The last time I told him not to contact me again, ever. He stopped. I finally felt free of guilt, and he never entered my mind. Two weeks ago, out of the blue, he called. In my mind we were never friends, so I was surprised he was looking for a shoulder to cry on.

He is now a colonel, and he said he was getting a divorce and his wife thought he was cheating. I asked, "Were you?"

His reply was, "Not really. I was just really close to someone. Sure, we went to dinner a lot because I am stationed far from home right now and we didn't want to move our kids out of school."

I listened for a while—I wish I hadn't—and he told me details of the divorce. His wife even went to his commanding officer about the affair. His commanding officer told her, if this was a pattern, they would have to address it.

I finally stopped him. I told him I couldn't listen. I was sad for his family and had to go. When he emailed, I asked him not to contact me again. Now I am going through all the guilt about being in an affair with a married man. I need to find my own peace, but that is a separate issue.

When I put myself in his wife's shoes, I would welcome any knowledge. I thought about contacting her. A friend of mine who has been through a cheating marriage encouraged me. A friend who is a psychologist says there is no right or wrong to telling, so do some soul-searching about whether to tell.

Part of me says suffer in silence and let it go. That is my lot for participating. Part of me says his wife should know. Her children and her life will be affected by the divorce and the knowledge will help. Yet it will hurt, too.

-Bree

Bree, this man didn't reappear to help you. He didn't come back to apologize for the negative impact he had on your life. He came back for his own purposes. He has himself to blame for picking up the phone to cry on your shoulder. The question is what are your purposes?

There are reasons you may want to tell. He lied to begin an affair with you, and you have self-loathing because of it. Now he has put in your way a chance to do what you could have done when he first approached you seven years ago: tell his wife. Telling the wife would say to him, "You cannot use me again without repercussions."

His wife, as far as you know, is blameless. She may be struggling with her decision to divorce. She may feel guilty about separating the family and making a claim on his military retirement. Coming forward would confirm the justness of her decision. In addition, the military has a code of honor and expects excellence, not deception, from senior officers.

There is a final reason to tell. It is not to our advantage to let people steal without being punished or cheat on exams. The only advantage goes to the cheater. For the rest of us in society, it is best for the cost of cheating to always outweigh the benefits. If he won't man-up and admit his actions, you can man-up for him.

-Wayne & Tamara

A woman in an uncomfortable spot writes:

Truth or Consequences

My husband's sister has been unfaithful to her husband for a couple of years. She made no secret about it to us and others, and her husband had an idea something was going on. I worked for her husband in a small office prior to my marriage to her brother, and I continue to work for him. I told my sister-in-law, if her husband ever asked me questions, I would be honest. I refuse to lie to my boss of 15 years.

Well, my boss (her husband and my brother-in-law) finally asked me if I knew what she was up to. I told him everything. My boss called his wife and confronted her. He told her where he got this information—something I didn't expect. She immediately called me and wanted to know if I was the one who gave her husband the information.

I was horrified when I realized I was caught in the middle. I told her, "No." Later, I told my husband what I had done. He was surprised, but when I reminded him we told his sister we would not lie if her husband asked questions, he seemed to understand. Please note my husband and his sister are very close.

The problem: everything seemed to blow over, but later I noticed my sister-in-law was treating me cruelly. (She does have a cruel streak, which I've witnessed her pull on her friends.) I mentioned this to my husband, and he said she probably still thinks I ratted her out.

Three months later, my husband tells me he told his sister I did, in fact, "rat her out." I now feel I can't trust my husband. We always had a "tell each other everything" relationship, but I don't feel that way anymore. I feel he chose his sister over me. I think that's wrong. Can you help me sort this out?

-Arielle

Arielle, when your sister-in-law confronted you, you had a split second to decide what to do, and you made the wrong decision. Your original decision, to tell the truth if confronted, was the right one. Otherwise you become an accomplice to cheating.

Having decided to tell the truth, you should have continued to tell the truth. What you failed to realize was one day you would have to stand up to your sister-in-law. Your husband followed the rule you both set up: if asked directly, tell the truth. The only person who fell out of that was you.

Emerson said, "If a man dissemble, deceive, he deceives himself, and goes out of acquaintance with his own being." If you stood up to your sister-in-law, it would have brought you some discomfort, but it was the only path to psychological freedom for you.

If your sister-in-law could count on your silence, it would only help her ignore her conscience. The more you blur the line between right and wrong, the more excuses people will make and the more people will be drawn over the line. Statements like "adultery doesn't end a marriage" allow some to think they can cheat and maintain their marriage. That statement disavows the consequences of cheating.

Cheating is a knowingly done misdeed. Removing the consequences encourages infidelity to occur. If professionals say stealing doesn't mean you have to go to jail, those who didn't steal out of fear of consequences will begin to steal. As Hegel said, "What the law permits, it encourages."

The more people accept the idea of cheating, the less value marriage has.

Don't expect good treatment from your sister-in-law. She doesn't treat her husband with respect. Don't let her actions come between you and your husband. He followed the path of honesty. He understood what you did in spite of his close connection to his sister. Understand what he did in spite of his close connection to you.

-Wayne & Tamara

Are there exceptions to our rule about telling? We can think of several:

- Telling should never be used as blackmail.
- Telling is pointless when the affected party already knows.
- Telling is inappropriate when the teller lacks direct knowledge.

The column below illustrates the last two exceptions.

Fish Food

Dan, my best friend, is dating Dawn and they have been together seven months. He is like a brother to me. He recently revealed plans to propose to Dawn, and he has officially asked her father's blessing. It is likely he will propose before the end of the year.

They dated briefly a year or two ago, but it ended when Dan discovered Dawn cheated on him. Ultimately, they repaired their problems and dove headfirst back into a relationship, with the understanding that this time they were going to commit fully or not commit at all.

Dan appears to be happy with the direction his life is heading. However, not all of Dan's friends approve of his relationship with Dawn, and even some of his family members have expressed reservations. I, too, struggle with the rapid rate at which they seem to be approaching marriage. I sometimes doubt Dawn's authenticity.

This past weekend, while spending time with friends from college, Claire, a close friend of Dan's and mine, informed me Dawn said unsettling things about her relationship with Dan and possibly cheated on him while out of town for work.

Claire learned Dawn met a guy at a bar and ended up sharing wine in her hotel room and talking to him all night. This, in itself, is not necessarily something Dan would need to know. However, it is not the end of the story. After telling me about the guy from the bar, Claire said she heard Dawn say she is not attracted to Dan but feels he can give her what she wants in life.

Unfortunately, I haven't heard or seen anything firsthand. Typically, when presented with information that could be disruptive or hurtful, I stay out of the situation and let things work themselves out without my intervention. I am struggling with that option in this case.

If I stay out of the situation, it is likely nothing will be said, and Dan will get engaged to Dawn. If I share this information with Dan, he will be hurt and take out his anger on Dawn, the potential offender, or me, the hesitant messenger.

Is there a right answer to this problem?

I would want a friend to tell me if I were in a similar situation, but part of me feels I was never meant to have this information, and maybe I should stay out of their relationship, trusting that what is meant to be will be.

-Luke

Luke, I was once sitting on the side of a small lake when a dragonfly flew straight in the water an arm's length away. I watched it thrash around for a minute or two before reaching in the water and rescuing it. I placed it on a flagstone to dry out. Five minutes later, fully recovered, it flew straight into the water at the exact same spot. A bass knifed to the surface and swallowed it whole.

Something like that is going on here, and you probably can't stop it.

We always say firsthand knowledge carries with it an obligation to act, but you don't have firsthand knowledge. What you have is hearsay. Those with firsthand knowledge cannot unburden themselves by telling you what they have heard. They cannot make you the fall guy. If they believe Dan should know what they know, it's up to them to tell him.

Dan has firsthand knowledge of Dawn. He knows Dawn cheated on him. He looks into her eyes. Let him decide whether to dive into the water in the same spot.

-Wayne

Things grow more complicated when the one discovering the affair is a child.

My Hands Are Tied

My oldest son has been married over 25 years. They have two girls, 26 and 24, and a son 13. He and his wife have substantial careers.

My son is wonderful to me and a good father, especially to his young son. Periodically I feel certain he has been unfaithful to his marriage. I suspect oth-

ers in our family know yet look the other way. Deep down, I thought his wife had to be aware at some level.

Inadvertently, a text meant for my son made it to him and his son's phone. It was obviously about an affair. His son did not understand it, so he showed it to one of his sisters. She, in turn, sent a long text to the other woman telling her off and telling her to leave her dad alone.

This sister also told her other sister. Now all three children are aware of something.

My son offered to pay for the college tuition of the daughter who responded to the text if she did not tell her mom. She hasn't. But the other sister, who works for my husband, recently broke down and told us the whole story.

We haven't said a word to my son. What should I do? I'm not okay with turning a blind eye. How do I approach my son, or would you advise me to mind my own business?

-Sondra

Sondra, raising children the message is, "This is right, that is wrong." Children get other rules too. Do your homework, turn down the music, tie your shoes, your hair is too long, and you are not going out of the house looking like that. It's only natural children will turn that same critical eye on their parents. There is nothing gray in a kid's life. They are not allowed to think, "I can get a little drunk..."

But as people get older, the world becomes gray. With the burdens of work and income, children, insurance, house payments, car payments, college funds, rising prices, and retirement accounts, not to mention the inner turmoil we have as we age, a feeling grows.

Where is my life?

So some people do things they shouldn't to get by. Corners get cut. Lies abound. An adult may think, "I work hard. I get to do things my kids should not do."

Perhaps your son felt his wife forced him into the marriage because she got pregnant. Perhaps he thought, "I was paying for the foal, I might as well live with the mare." Perhaps that's the way he felt for most or all of the marriage.

There is right and there is wrong, but wrong has a thumb on the scale. Wrong has "but" on its side. But she's so hot, but I want that job, but I can use the money. As we get older, all our buts get bigger.

You assumed your daughter-in-law knew. Maybe that was self-defense on your part. If she knew, you did not need to act. But you've jumped out of that camp because your son's bribe to a daughter proves his wife does not know. Your excuse has vanished. How much worse will it be when your daughter-in-law learns everyone in the family knew the secret but her? She will feel betrayed by everyone.

Your son has given you no choice. You can't let him make you an accomplice to his duplicity. Tell your daughter-in-law what you know.

-Wayne & Tamara

In the letter above, a 13-year-old boy got a text he didn't understand, so he asked his adult sister what it meant. That started a chain of events, but it doesn't address a central question. What are the effects of cheating on children? That's the topic for the next chapter. But first, we haven't given you our answer to the woman who became part of the 'collection' of a serial adulterer.

This is our reply to her.

Elise, just as he acted as if he has the free will to deceive and betray his spouse, just as he acted as if he has the free will to deceive the women he ensnares, so each of those women has free will of their own. They have the right to tell the wife and anyone else they care to tell.

The man you were involved with doesn't own the knowledge of his affairs. Others know, and at any time any of them may tell. At all times, each of them is free to tell. Telling is merely the price of his adultery.

We always advise telling. The spouse has the right to know. The spouse has the right to know everything their life partner is involved in. In addition, telling may protect other women from becoming his next victim.

Cheaters should be known by their actions. That's no more than simple honesty. It's the price a person pays for doing wrong. The affair partner has not taken some kind of tacit oath not to tell. When the cheater dumps his partner in adultery, that person is free to dump on him.

The man you were involved with was not so miserably married he was getting a divorce, but he claimed he was "miserably married" as an excuse to cheat. The logic simply doesn't hold.

What you learned says it all: "...the tangents of damage and pain that have been caused by his behavior have become serious reverberating ripples throughout all of our lives and have, without question, left permanent scars on our souls."

We couldn't agree more.

-Wayne & Tamara

CHAPTER 14
CHEATING: EFFECTS ON CHILDREN

"Don't worry that children never listen to you;
worry that they are always watching you."
—Robert Fulghum, best-selling author

After surveying the literature on how cheating affects children, law professor Lynn Wardle concluded the "comforting notion that what children do not see will not hurt them is false. Even if children do not see the adulterous acts, like children who do not witness one parent openly beat the other, they see wounds inflicted upon the victim-spouse and perceive the pain and suffering that one parent has caused the other." Wardle says, "Even if the children do not know the details of the affair, they see the consequences, they experience the loss of trust, and they share in the suffering and the despair of the betrayal."[1]

We agree, and in this chapter, we let the voices of children with a cheating parent speak.

A girl writes:

I am a 15-year-old girl from a Chinese Singaporean family. My family is generally okay, not exactly warm and loving, but adequate. When I was 11, I found out my mother was cheating on my father with a doctor who I knew and trusted.

I've kept quiet about the affair for years, but it remains a weight on me, refusing to disappear with the passage of time. I don't know why I am this upset.

Is it really something that concerns me? It isn't. The only people involved in the affair are my mother, her lover, and my father. Is it my right to be as upset as I am?

I have started scratching and cutting my wrist with a penknife. It is not as dramatic as some people would have it sound. The ritual brings me some peace, some sense of isolation, and some sense of relief. I see it as a coping method. My mother does not know that I know about her affair or that I cut myself. It hurts. So please, would you tell me what to do?

-Hua

Another girl writes:

A few years ago, I learned my father was cheating on my mom. I was sleeping in my parents' room, and my younger siblings and I had just come home from school. Because my parents' room is the most comfortable, I decided to nap there.

I was already in a deep sleep when my mother came into the room. She was back from work. Not long after, my father came home too. To this day I can't recall the beginning of their argument, nor can I stop wondering how they did not notice I was there. Perhaps they simply didn't care at that point.

My mom told my father she was positive for some STD and accused him of cheating, because, God knows, throughout their 15 years of marriage she remained faithful. My father told my mom he loved another woman and wished to be with her. My mom told him to go if he wanted, but she would want a divorce. My father disagreed saying he didn't want his family to break up.

At that point I had the urge to yell, but I pretended to sleep. How dare my father say that? He was never there. He wasn't there at sports day when I won a prize, he wasn't there for my ballet recital, and he wasn't there when I received a prize for placing first in my year group.

My mom was always there, and if she wasn't, she had a damn good reason. She cooked, cleaned, worked, played with us and tucked us in at night. But

130

as great a mother as she was, it could never fill the gap of not having my father there. That moment was also when I found out my mother was pregnant. I was as shocked as my father was when she told him. I can't recall what happened after that. I think I just blacked out or walked out of the room. It was too much for a 12-year-old.

Later, my mom asked my dad to leave. In his hotel room my father explained he did something bad to my mother and regretted it. But as much as we asked, he wouldn't say what it was. I thought my father was a coward then because he couldn't even tell the truth.

It's been a couple of years now. My parents decided to try to mend their marriage, but the whole situation is one big fat elephant in the room. Sometimes I have the urge to yell at my father when he scolds me over some minor matter.

When people ask do I want to get married, I always say no. They ask why, and I say because I don't want to. But I know the real reason. I'm scared. I never want to experience what my mom did. Sometimes I just want to snap.

-Katie

One man, the father of girls aged four and one, learned of his wife's affair when he walked into a room and her email was up. That email exposed six months of duplicity. The other man was a divorced dad whose daughters went to the same gym as his older daughter. He learned his wife arranged play dates for the girls while he was away on business and slept with the other man in their bed. On one occasion, after his eldest daughter caught them in bed at night, his wife and her lover convinced the child she had been dreaming.

An international businessman told us his wife used their 12-year-old son to pass messages between herself and her lover. She swore the boy and his brother, five, to secrecy, and told them not to utter the other man's name in their father's presence. To avoid sleeping with him when he came home from a trip, the wife would claim, "The kids want to sleep with Daddy." When she couldn't avoid sharing a bed with him, she put their youngest son between them.

On one of the 15 or so business trips he took each year, his wife's behavior was so peculiar he called the maid and asked if she was having an affair. The maid confirmed it. Rushing home unannounced one morning, he found a closetful of clothes, not his size, in the bedroom. His wife locked herself in the bathroom and made frantic phone calls trying to devise a cover story.

Knowledge of an affair always creates conflict and dysfunction in children. It often forces the child to make a choice between parents, and the only power a child has to resolve this conflict is by confronting one or both parents.

A young woman writes:

Shortly after my 17th birthday my parents called me and my brother, who is two years younger, into the living room for a family meeting. I always hated that because it meant something bad was about to happen.

My parents sat us down and explained they were separating because they were just too different or some bull crap like that. I had seen it coming but my brother not so much. It's been a month, school started, and we made it work. Our parents weren't going to make us choose. We came and went from each house as we pleased. Recently my dad found out that before him and my mom separated, my mom was cheating with a man she met at a concert.

I never would have expected this from her. She always instilled these ideas into me about right and wrong, and here she is being a hypocrite. She tried to contact me and my brother, but we've ignored her.

I'm just so angry. I will never accept this guy, whoever he is. He may be nice, but because he disregarded that he knew my mom was married and still dated her, I will never welcome him into the family. I'm sad to say my mom and this dude totally disrespected my dad, and that's not okay with me. I know she's my mom and all, but as of right now I don't want anything to do with her.

-Gretchen

British relationship author Kate Figes, writing in the *Daily Mail*, categorized the harms done to the children of cheaters by age.[2]

- Young children may miss out on cuddling, eye contact, and attention.
- Five to ten-year-olds are more likely to think they cause their parents' problems. They may have nightmares and show regressive behavior, like bedwetting or thumb sucking.
- Older teens and young adults may display destructive behavior, get depressed or sick, or stop eating.

Figes quotes sociologist Jean Duncombe, who says, "Some parents seem to think that once their children have gone to university, it doesn't matter anymore because they're adults. But they're still children within that context. So they're absolutely devastated. It's the lies, I think, that cause the deepest damage."

Jean Duncombe's view is echoed in the following letter.

Usually people ask me for advice, but this time around, I don't know what to do. I'm 21 and living a continent away from my parents who are getting divorced. It started last year, when they decided to start marriage counseling. I was fine with this. My parents had problems for as long as I could remember, and I thought they were finally taking the first step toward fixing things.

Sometime in between their decision to see a marriage counselor and actually going to the counselor, my father started cheating.

Learning this was hard. My father instilled a strong sense of justice in me, and he always held to a black-and-white type of law, not the gray-scale.

It shook me to my core, especially since I had always been a bit of a daddy's girl. It hurt even more to realize he'd been lying to me over Skype.

I was angry and made sure he felt it. After my initial blowup at him, I've been civil. But every time I talk with him or think of him, I get depressed or feel nauseous, as though the mere thought of his presence makes me ill.

Now he's said he has a conference in a place near where I'm living, a place I've always wanted to see. I said yes, originally, and we agreed to go for two weeks. But now plans need to be made, dates set, hotels booked, and I find myself dreading it.

Part of me knows this will be a good way to try and move past this. A very strong part of me says, "No, don't go." I feel it will be horrible to go, to have to see that sickening, lying, traitorous, hypocritical face every day, all day.

I don't know if I can do it. But I know he will see that as the ultimate rejection, which it is, and it may end with us never mending a broken relationship.

-Devon

In the following letter, a young woman, for reasons she doesn't understand, seems on the path to replicate the behavior of her cheating father.

I'm a 21-year-old girl. My father cheated on my mom growing up, and I couldn't bear to visit him because I couldn't bear to look at the lady he cheated with. I felt I was betraying my mom.

My mom married a wonderful man who took the place of my real dad. Weekend visits with my real dad ended because he didn't want to see me after I asked my stepdad to adopt me.

Now I am in my first relationship that began when I was 20 in college. He is the perfect guy. Oh my, is he perfect in every way. But feeling secure about this makes me disrespect it. I still talk to other guys and even kiss them.

Why do I do this when I know how much my real dad hurt my mom?

-Tabitha

As we told Tabitha, when you make a choice for yourself as a parent, you often make a choice for your children. That's what happened to her. Adultery in her parents' marriage affected her life and her relationships. When a parent suffers a trauma, so does the child. Glenn Schiraldi calls these downstream effects intergenerational secondary wounding.[3] A parent's problem is passed to the children.

Having an affair requires wining and dining, plotting and scheming, flirting and prioritizing. Think back to when you were dating. Think how time-consuming it was to establish a relationship—texting, phoning, exchanging pictures and emojis.

In cheating, time, attention, and money are taken away from children. A cheater often acts like their affair partner is in a box, in another dimension, and the affair isn't affecting "my real life." But when a cheater puts their partner at risk, they also put their own offspring at risk. Cheating may lead to the breakup of the marriage, the breakup of the household, and the breakup of the relationship with the children.

The next letter, from an adult man, is about the so-called sleeper effect, the effects of parental cheating, which show up after a child grows into adulthood.[4]

I am a male, 42. My mother cheated on my father with our family doctor. The doctor's surgery was next door to my parents' shop, and she used to go next door at lunch to chat with the doctor, who became a family friend.

This lasted three years before Dad found out. The family fell apart. Dad sold everything and moved to England, where he found another family and barely had contact with me. Mum moved in with a guy unconnected to the breakup.

Every time I start to have feelings for a girl, I find a reason to end it. I feel my mother has ruined my mind and my core trust of females.

-Curt

An adult woman writes:

I am married to a good husband, with two awesome children. I am an only child from parents who were 21 when they had me. They were not married until a year after I was born. I am fine with that, but I was never told. I found out by trying on my mom's wedding band and looking at the dates inside.

I worshipped my parents. They were always cool parents because they were the youngest, hippest parents around when I was growing up, but now, as a parent, I realize being hip is not important.

Both my parents had affairs. I believe it was more than one for both of them. My mom does not know I know. I do not want to feel angry but I am. Because of their selfishness I missed out on having parents around me when I needed it most.

I remember being picked up after every kid at school—sitting in the parking lot by myself for what seemed like hours. My parents let me get away with unacceptable behavior. I had no boundaries, and nobody seemed to give a hoot about what I really needed—guidance, leadership, and TLC.

I want to be the best wife, mom, daughter, and friend to all around me, but I don't want to hear what my parents have to say anymore. I do not understand how people have time for affairs unless they neglect other things, and while I sit here, I feel they neglected me.

I would not say that to anyone, but I needed them during all those years. I needed them at track meets. I needed them to talk to me about how I should behave with boys and how drinking is not cool. Now I remember things I do not want to remember. How can I heal because I do not want to feel sorry for myself?

-Dusty

And one final letter, from our column.

Just Desserts

My father is estranged from my sister and me. When we were very young, he and my mother divorced. He did not pay child support or anything. Recently he came back into town and wants a relationship with us. He says he's changed. He says he is a Christian. He wants to get to know my sister and me better and be allowed to share in his grandchildren's lives.

As my sister and I are getting used to the idea of giving him a second chance, he admits to all of us he cheated on our mother repeatedly while they were married. He finally tells us he is presently involved with one of the women he had an affair with, and he hopes we'll get to know her and accept their relationship.

We told him this was too much for us to deal with. He thinks we're being selfish. Are my sister and I wrong for not being willing to accept this?

-Paula

Paula, the most basic law of behavior is the law of consequences. If you don't study, you will fail the exam. In Christian terms, this law is expressed by "As you sow, so shall you reap." Your father is reaping what he sowed.

Justice means balancing the scales. Things should be fair. There is no fairness in what your biological father is asking. He wants to reap the benefits of having daughters and grandchildren when he was not there for you physically, emotionally, or financially. Justice does not require you to let him into your life or the lives of your children.

Perhaps you believe there is a higher requirement than justice, forgiveness. Then by all means forgive, because forgiveness releases us from the pain and hurt which bind us. However, nothing in the idea of forgiveness requires you to let someone who has injured you into your life so they can injure you again. If forgiveness required that, you would never be permitted to escape people who do bad acts, and your life would be forfeited to them.

137

There is someone selfish here, and that someone is your biological father. He wants to use religion as a club to get his own way. The decision you and your sister made is just. It is in tune with the deepest law of behavior, the law of consequences.

-Wayne & Tamara

The effects of cheating on children are profound. Cheating has far-reaching consequences people don't see and some don't want you to see. And there are even more effects on the partner of an unfaithful person than we have mentioned. We'll talk about them next.

CHAPTER 15
EFFECTS ON YOU

"Sometimes a tie that is not worth preserving is kept alive by giving in too readily to the demands of others—or by accepting apologies for unacceptable behavior."

—Frans de Waal, primatologist

I found out last December that my husband of six years cheated on me and had been for almost two years. The only reason I found out was because the psycho he was cheating on me with smashed his windshield. He tried to lie at first and say he didn't know who did it, and then finally, after two days, he told me who did it but said she was just 'obsessed' with him.

I did some investigating on my own and even called her and confronted her. She told me she was having an affair with him. So I confronted him and he stuck with his story. I made him take a lie detector test, and it came out that he was being purposefully deceitful. So I did some more investigating and got a hotel receipt from one of the nights she said they were together.

Then I confronted him again. He denied it until I would not let up. I was crushed and my faith and trust in him was destroyed. After a few days I finally listened to his apologies and we talked, and I cried and I stayed. I didn't want to because I have always said I would not be with a cheater. But we have a three-year-old son together, and I just couldn't see him growing up without his dad being there every day.

But now it's been almost a year and I still cannot get over it and I know I never will. I still cry and have days when it's all I can think about. He swears it will never happen again and that he has re-devoted himself to me. I do love him, but I told him I will never love him the way I once did, and I will never trust him the way I did. I want to stay but I don't know if I'm being naïve.

He doesn't understand why I still get upset and says, "What can I do? What have I done wrong now?" and, "I regret what I did every day." I think he does but I don't see him losing sleep or falling apart and crying like I do. How can I heal and try to make my marriage work and regain some of the trust I used to have in him? I want to make it work. I have 10 years in this relationship and we now have two children together. I don't want my kids growing up with divorced parents...they deserve to have both of us there for them every day.

-Wendi

A woman in her 60s told us she divorced her philandering husband decades ago. Then she read an article about a woman who discovered her husband had a mistress. She started crying then grew angry. "Why?" she asks. "I'm not going through anything like that, but I absorbed her pain, then, to top it off, I have been constantly reading everything I can get my hands on about affairs. I am always left in such a wrecked-up state emotionally."

In this chapter, we will focus on two things: the nature of loss in betrayal and the nature of stigma.

Robert Cooter, a University of California law professor, explains the law recognizes two kinds of loss, compensable and incompensable.[1] Compensable losses are easy to understand and accept. I drive while texting, lose control, and plow through your fence. To compensate you, I must either restore the fence to its original condition or give you enough money to have it repaired. You suffered an economic loss, and it's easy to calculate and pay for economic damages.

Incompensable loss is another matter. I drive while texting, lose control, and kill your child. That loss is incompensable. Your child is beyond market value. Cooter says trying to calculate damages in this case is like asking someone to "find a sum of money such that the parents are indifferent between having a dead child and the money, or having a living child and no money." The thought itself is sickening because there is no point at which the choice is a tossup.

If someone cheats on you, you've been changed. The wholeness of your relationship is lost, the pristineness gone, and perhaps a vow broken. You are out that initial promise. We have talked about this issue before, but we haven't named it. Incompensable loss is its name. The question a victim of cheating must face is whether they have suffered an incompensable loss and whether some leveling will ever be possible in their relationship.

If it's a marriage, another's actions broke a contract. Do you want to renegotiate? Do you want to set a new contract with this person? Would you marry this person again or set a penalty? Their promise not to do it again doesn't level anything. It's hot air. A promise not to do what they already promised not to do is meaningless. It doesn't undo what was done. The offending party isn't going to talk about compensatory damages because what can he or she give you? What will get rid of this sullied mess?

In ancient Greece, a mark was burned into the skin of people who were disgraced or tainted, like criminals and traitors. That mark was called a stigma. Today, stigma still attaches to people in some circumstances. Though the mark is invisible, it is real. If you stay with a cheater, their transgression taints you, even though you had no hand in it. If a man stays with a cheating woman, he is viewed as weak. If a woman stays with a man who cheats, she is seen as a woman who can't hold a man's attention. It's a form of guilt by association, but it is very real.

Stigma may also explain why some psychologists, counselors, or psychiatrists blame the victim as well as the cheater and tell the victim to "take your part in this."

Staying with a cheater sullies the one who stays. Research demonstrates that people assume someone in a certain role wanted the role, even when they had no choice in the matter.[2] For example, in one experiment, politicians were randomly assigned to read speeches for or against a topic.[3] Even though observers were told the speaker was assigned the speech by chance, they still believed the speaker favored the position that was assigned to them.

What you are connected to, even when it involves no fault on your part, will cause people to reevaluate your character, traits, and beliefs. Lie down with dogs, get up with fleas, says an old adage.

Risk expert Paul Slovic remarks that people who are stigmatized are thought to "have attributes that do not accord with prevailing standards of the normal and good."[4] Being stigmatized blocks communication with others and makes you less desirable to be around. If you stay with a cheater, you won't sell the happy ending to friends and relatives who know about the cheating. Even if they don't roll their eyes, they won't believe you. If you tell only a few people, the circle of knowledge will grow wider than you realize.

Who should pay for that? The one who put the relationship at risk. There are very few things which in and of themselves kill a marriage. The main premise of marriage, or a serious relationship, is that it's you and me and no one else. Cheating destroys that premise.

A Bed of Nails

I'm not sure why I am writing. I guess I just need to talk. When I was in my early 20s, I was deeply and utterly in love, and I married a wonderful person.

After 11 years and two children, I found out my wife had an ongoing relationship with another man. I would say affair, but I don't think that does it justice. You see my wife's affair started five months after we married and continued 11 years. When I found out, I was devastated and wanted to leave her. Looking back, I should have.

The affair stopped, she apologized, and I changed. My kids, my wife, and our home were my life. I learned you don't just stop loving someone when you find out this type of thing. It takes three or four years, but eventually it happens.

I told no one but my dad. I told him I would stay with her for the kids, but it was really for me. I wanted to prove to her she had made a mistake. Now, seven years later, my kids are bigger and happy, we never talk about the situation, and I have become a very sad person. I spend a lot of time wondering if the kids are mine.

The life and relationship I was trying not to lose is gone. I'm left with a nice person who I care for, but it's not the same. I want to be in love the way I used to be, the way she must have been with the other man. I really don't need an answer. It was nice, almost therapeutic, to be able to express my feelings.

-Basil

Basil, your silence is the only thing holding the situation together now. Writing made you feel better, but in a little while the effect will wear off and you will be left where you were. When that happens, you will seek to take another step.

Now you are doing nothing proactive. Are you going to wonder for the rest of your life if the children are yours? What if they are? Then you will have wondered for nothing and, at least unconsciously, shown you doubt your connection to them.

Children are the emotional barometer of a marriage. To think they are ever fooled about the state of their parents' marriage is a mistake. Finding out can allay some of your fears. If they are not your biological children, you won't abandon your fatherly role, but at least you will end the uncertainty.

Underneath your sadness there must be a great deal of anger because nothing, absolutely nothing, allows for what your wife did to you. While you remain silent, you must conceal your anger. Until those feelings come out you won't know what to do with your life.

Ultimately you have to decide how much of your life and its possibilities your wife is allowed to determine. Step by step you will find your answer.

-Wayne & Tamara

Finding the love of your life is for many people the greatest life task of all. Unlike Basil, after discovery some people go right to "I'm done." Perhaps they weren't close to their partner, or perhaps they have a sense of self-worth that will not allow them to stay. Perhaps they think, *How dare you!* Whatever the case, almost instantly they jump to the spot where they are ready to start healing and move on.

The man below, writing from Texas, appeared to grasp all the implications of betrayal in under 24 hours.

Yesterday, I caught my girlfriend of two years in bed with my now ex-friend. I walked in and caught them in the act. After beating the hell out of him, I told my girlfriend to go to our house and wait for me. Upon arriving home, the question I kept asking is, "Why?" She says she doesn't know why.

We went and saw a counselor that very same day. I told her we could work through this, but after sleeping on it I'm not sure I want to.

-Roy

Roy, most people who sleep on a problem wake up just as muddled as they were the night before. But in the course of one night, you gained the insight needed to grasp the end of your relationship. Why do you go to work? Why do you pay your bills? Why do you lock your truck in a bad neighborhood? You know why.

When someone is caught doing what they know is wrong, the classic first answer is, "I don't know why." Why do they say that? Because once you admit guilt, you must suffer consequences. If you claim ignorance, there is a chance you might escape justice.

Ultimately, why doesn't matter. What she did ended the relationship. What she did trumps why she did it.

-Wayne & Tamara

"I don't know why" is not a great answer, but cheaters who use it know it is better than the truth.[5] If Roy's girlfriend said what she thought and why she gave herself the right, the relationship would be over.

Of those who stay with a cheater, many end up in what psychologist Scott Plous refers to as a deterioration trap.[6] The classic deterioration trap is heroin addiction. In the beginning, using the drug is highly pleasurable. As users keep using, they build up a tolerance and need to use more heroin to get the same high. Eventually, they keep using not to get high but to avoid the agony of withdrawal. They are stuck in a state of dependence.

Relationships can deteriorate in the same way. In the aftermath of cheating, the couple continues in a way that appears irrational to outsiders. They have fights that never settle anything, they keep hoping for an improvement that never comes, and they ignore the insights of others. It's as if they have a drug habit they cannot kick.

As we turn to Chapter 16, we would like you to bear one thing in mind. Reconciliation can be self-defeating.[7]

CHAPTER 16
WHAT TO DO NOW

*"I feel there are two people inside me—me and my intuition.
If I go against her, she'll screw me every time, and if I follow
her, we get along quite nicely."*

—Kim Basinger, actress

If you have been cheated on, you face one central question. What do I do now?

We consider two things obligatory. We'll mention them first. Then we'll mention what else you might do.

Whether you go or stay, the first thing you need to do is get a full range of tests for sexually transmitted infections. It doesn't matter if your partner says the affair was only emotional, they used protection, it only happened once, or they just kissed. This is about protecting yourself from someone who didn't care enough about protecting you.

Examinations for sexually transmitted infections may include tests for gonorrhea, chlamydia, syphilis, HIV/AIDS, herpes (HSV), trichomoniasis, hepatitis, and human papillomavirus (HPV), among others. Many sexually transmitted infections have no signs or symptoms, and the cost of neglecting testing and treatment for some of these infections is severe. You can do testing at a private physician's office, a neighborhood women's clinic, or a public health clinic.

When you sleep with your boyfriend or husband, girlfriend or wife, you sleep with everyone he or she has ever slept with and everyone they slept with. That's why you need to be tested, and probably more than once, because some complications of sexually transmitted infections only show up in time.

Our second mandatory recommendation is for those in a relationship with commingled assets. Privately, you need to consult a good attorney. By privately we mean an attorney outside your social and business circles and without the knowledge of your partner. An initial consult is often free.

If you are married, a party with whom you have a contractual relationship has broken the contract. Psychologists, psychiatrists, counselors, therapists, priests, ministers, imams, and rabbis have one thing in common. They are not competent to give legal advice. Someone has breached a contract and put you in an unstable, high-risk legal quandary. You need to know where you stand in the event of a divorce or separation. Only an attorney can answer these questions and help you develop a legal strategy.

If you are not married but have significant commingled assets with your partner—cars, boats, homes, farms, lines of credit, and bank accounts—you also need to see an attorney. You need to know where you stand, and you need a strategy for unraveling your assets from theirs.

A medical examination and a legal consultation, if you have common assets, are the minimum of what you must do. But you should do more. Consider all your options. Considering your options is the only thing that will put power into your hands. Someone acted upon you. Now it is your turn to decide what your life will be. That alone has the power to free you from a victim mentality.

Psychologist Robert Cialdini notes that people typically try to act in a way consistent with their past decisions. That suggests, if you have been in a relationship, you may stay simply to remain consistent with what you have done in the past. Instead, Cialdini suggests two other ways of looking at the problem.[1]

Stomachs, he says, are not very sensitive instruments, but they can warn us when we are about to make a bad decision. So ask yourself, on a gut level, what feels like the right thing to do? Alternatively, you might consult your heart of hearts. Ask yourself, what does my heart tell me to do?

The gut test and the heart of hearts test are two signals, right from your own body, that can help you decide whether to leave. Rationalizations, slogans, and clichés don't reside in either place. These two methods correspond with an observation cardiologist Alan Watkins made in his book *Coherence*.[2] Negative feelings center in the neural system around the gut, while positive feelings center in the neural system around the heart.

A woman writes:

Hello, I married a man I'm not in love with and have never been in love with. Deep down I knew it was wrong from the beginning. Now I have recently fallen in love with someone other than my husband. This is the first time I've been in love, and I'm 31 years old.

I've been married for two and a half years, with no children. Now that I'm actually in love, I realized that I married my husband with the HOPE of falling in love with him. I really liked him, but wasn't sure if I loved him or not.

I also didn't get to know him well enough before marrying him. I only knew him for four months before getting married. Then I found out that he was not at all the person I thought he was. I know I made a colossal mistake, and would like to set things right, but how do you tell your spouse that you want a divorce and in fact never loved him? Also, how do you forgive yourself for making such a huge, stupid mistake in the first place?

-Leah

Leah's letter is a reminder that the discovery of cheating is the perfect time to honestly examine why you got married.

A man writes:

The reason it took so long to tie the knot was because I didn't feel she was the right one. She apparently fell in love with me on our first date, but I didn't feel the same way. After our second date, I told her I wanted to date other women, and I broke up with her. A couple of weeks went by, and I couldn't stop think-ing about how I had broken her heart, so I called her. After more breakups, he says: The last time I gave up and asked her to marry me, since I was unable to be firm and tell her we were through. I know that was stupid. I'd hate to know I'm the only person who has ever done that.

-Wolfe

He's not. In fact, it's a plot element in Sinclair Lewis' 1922 satirical novel *Babbitt*. People enter relationships for many wrong reasons. That's why, after cheating is discovered, it pays to go back and examine the rea-son you entered the relationship and act from that knowledge.

Ask most people why they married and they will say, "It was love." But that is not always true. The oldest reason is, "We had sex and she got pregnant." Others marry for money and social position. A woman might say, "He was the first person to ask, I wanted the big wedding," or, "All my friends were getting married."

Some marry to have children or because their parents pressured them for grandchildren. Others want to escape their parents' house. Still others would say, "He asked and I didn't know how to say no," or, "I couldn't explain why we shouldn't get married." And for some, it's because their culture believes in arranged marriage.

Yet other people believed marriage would change the other person or fix their relationship. And some just wanted someone, anyone. Finally, many people are together because they mistook infatuation for love.

Another way to answer the "What should I do now?" question is to use zero-based thinking. Zero-based thinking asks, "If I knew then what I know now, would I have involved myself with this person?" As time man-agement expert Brian Tracy says, "What is the purpose of a relationship? The simplest answer is so you'll be happier than you would be if you were not in that relationship at all. This is so obvious that it is overlooked by many people."

In his book *Time Power*, Tracy observes, "The choice of the right relationship can have more of an impact on your happiness than any other choice you make. The choice of a wrong relationship can do more to destroy your hopes and dreams than any other choice."[3]

People commonly talk about having two years or 15 years or 40 years "invested in this relationship." Calling it an investment is economic language, and an economist would suggest that you consider the opportunity cost. If you choose to stay, you are excluding all the benefits you might receive from a different course of action.

Cognitive psychologist Gary Klein offers a third way to look at your decision making.[4] Most of us know that a postmortem examination is performed to determine a cause of death. Klein suggests people can make more informed decisions by conducting what he calls a "premortem" examination. In a premortem examination, you consider a worst-case scenario.

In relationships, a premortem might look like this. Imagine it is a year after your decision to stay. The year has been wretched. Now list the reasons why. It might help to enlist the help of a trusted friend or other person, who is your advocate, to generate a fuller list.

Items that might be on your list are:

- We did the counseling, and six months later it was the same old story.
- I felt I never got the truth from her.
- He's angry every time I bring up his cheating.
- I could never get over my feelings.
- I would not listen to my friends and family who told me I deserved better.

- Staying with her forced me to live a public lie to maintain appearances.
- I agreed to counseling out of politeness and good manners, but it was a waste.
- I will never trust him.

The premortem exam doesn't just help identify potential problems. It injects realism into the decision-making process.

I am at the most painful place I have ever been in my life. I have been married for just over 10 years and have four children. What I don't have is a faithful or honest husband. I have made the decision to leave this marriage since he has not spent any time trying to create a long-lasting marriage and has, in fact, systematically set up secret identities and email addresses to conduct encounters with both women and men. I can't stay with him. I have filed papers and we are going through everything 'amicably.'

However, I am having second thoughts about the 'amicable' part of this. I have a mix of emotions. I am devastated and haven't been able to figure out what to make of my life now. I feel like it's been stolen from me by the one person I should have been able to trust more than any other. I am dealing with children who miss their father's daily presence terribly, but I can't tell them why and they feel I forced this on them and that I am to blame.

They still love him, and I don't want to hurt that relationship for them. But I am stressed out. My nerves are raw. I still have intense feelings for him, and it is like the intellectual knowledge that this relationship is over won't sink through to the heart. And seconds later I feel immense rage and near hatred towards him for causing me this pain. Then there is the terrible depression and fear of this type of thing ever occurring again.

What do I do now? How can I make sure I never go through this again? A lot of friends suggest that I cut him out of my life completely. I really want to do this too...I think I need to be away from him to calm this emotional maelstrom. But I am mostly afraid of whether the kids will still love me or understand why we don't do anything together anymore, especially since I promised them that both of us would be there for their sports, drama, birthdays, and other activities.

-Summer

Children often factor into the decision to stay, though, as we saw in Chapter 14, whether staying contributes to their well-being is dubious. Staying may set them up for future relationship failures.

About six and a half years ago, I was shocked and devastated to discover my husband had been having a six-month affair with a coworker. I was a stay-at-home mom with three small children at the time. His reason? He wanted someone to pay attention to him but failed to mention to me that he thought I was neglecting him!

We decided to stay together and try to work things out. Looking back, I can see that part of the reason I agreed to this was that I was very afraid to be on my own and felt like no one else would want me with three children. I have always had difficulty with low self-esteem, but I have also struggled with thoughts that I betrayed myself and compromised my personal beliefs by remaining married after the affair.

This past fall, my oldest child went away to school and I began a new career, teaching. Just about everything my husband does seems to annoy me...I have basically concluded that I deserve so much better and I may be better off actually being alone. The thing that tears me up is the effect it will have on our three children if we split up. However, I have been concerned that we are not providing a good example of what a good marriage is like.

-Angela

In order to make a wise decision, our advice is to escape from the slogans, clichés, and platitudes about relationships. You must make your own decision based on information that matters. Yet much research confirms that people make decisions based on superfluous information.

For example, in one experiment, people were asked to estimate the year Attila the Hun was defeated in Europe.[5] But first they were asked to add 400 to the last three digits of their phone number. The resulting number strongly correlated with their estimates for the date of Attila's defeat. In another experiment, people wrote down the last two numbers on their social security card then bid on items in an auction. The group with higher numbers bid 60–120% higher than the group with lower numbers.[6]

Experiments like this have been done countless times. The vast majority of people are convinced they aren't influenced by irrelevant information, but they are.

Many people carry around one or more of the following beliefs:

- Everyone deserves a second chance.
- To err is human, to forgive is divine.
- We must save the marriage.
- I don't believe in divorce.
- God is in your marriage.
- Love is a decision.
- We can't judge other people.

All these statements are questionable. "You can't judge other people" is one of our favorites. The statement itself is absurd. Our lives are nothing but judgments. Each time you get into an automobile you make judgments. Should I turn or wait for an oncoming car to pass? Should I speed up or slow down? If you break down your day into separate acts, you will see it is composed of nothing but hundreds and thousands of judgments. Do I hire this man or that woman? Should I let this person into my home?

Furthermore, most of the major life judgments we make are black and white, not gray. Go to this school or that one. Major in biology or English. Marry him or break up with him.

In a similar way, each of the other statements can be shown, with a little thought, to be unsubstantiated. For example, if a man marries a woman for money, is God in that marriage? If a woman marries a man to beat her younger sister to the altar, what part did God play in that?

As a final test of whether to stay or go, we suggest the simplest test of all. If you had a daughter or a son who had been cheated on, what would you advise them to do?

What if the world went silent? What if there was no sound? Look at your dating, living together, or marriage relationship without audio. Without words, without excuses, without promises of future good behavior, just by yourself, make your decision. You are the only one who must live with it.

CHAPTER 17
ACCEPT

"You don't have to make money back the same way you lost it."
—Warren Buffett, legendary investor

My story, like most others, is all the signs are there, but for some reason I want to believe the lies. My recently ex-boyfriend has met his ex-wife behind my back, and I suspected an affair with his boss. So one night, when he was away and it was nagging me, I looked up her address. And low and behold his car was parked in her driveway at four in the morning.

He says he just left his car there for convenience while he went with friends for the night. I stayed with him another year and a half and had his son. There have been many other signs, such as him calling the same women from my bedroom while I bathed, about six months after we were to work things out.

I guess "Why?" is the question you get the most. But I don't want to know why he did all these things to me, but why did I stay with someone who would cheat on me and why would I want to believe the lies so much that I would go against my own logic?

-Rebecca

Another letter:

What do I do when I know my husband is a liar and a cheater but he refuses to discuss it? How can we work out our problems if he continues to deny he's done anything wrong? He thinks you should never admit to anything and if we don't talk about it, hopefully it will go away.

He has told me to get over it and get on with my life. That to me doesn't sound like he wants a future with me. He does whatever he wants with no regard for my feelings. I don't think he has any idea that he's pushing me further and further away. He's only making things worse by not telling the truth. I'll never trust him again. Help!

-Kelsi

A third letter, this one with our answer:

Ten years ago, I discovered a condom in my husband's jacket pocket. I assumed he was having an affair at work. On confronting him, he admitted to sex with prostitutes. He was devastated he had hurt me and, of course, I was never meant to find out.

I tried to understand it from his point of view. We didn't have sex often, mostly because he was cold toward me, bossy and critical. Just when I had enough and threatened to leave, he would soften and things would settle down for a while. This cycle went on for years.

I went for counseling to explain both sides of the picture, as he made me feel it was my fault we weren't getting on. I must have been mad. Two years ago, shortly before my mother died of cancer, I discovered I had genital herpes, and my husband moved into the spare room.

I assumed he was having sex with prostitutes, though he assured me he was faithful. I wanted to believe him, but I never really trusted him after the first disclosure. I should have left or made him leave, but I felt powerless. Three months later, I looked up sex addiction on the internet. After reading many articles I felt this was my husband's problem.

I wrote him a letter saying I would stand by him if he admitted this was the problem. One evening, he asked me to come into his room. He was pale and shivering. He disclosed 15 years of sex addiction—sex with men in parks and public toilets, prostitutes, and an affair.

I was living in a nightmare you can't wake up from. He made an appointment with a psychiatrist the day after he told me, and I went for more counseling. We went for couples counseling, he started seeing a psychologist, and now we are seeing the psychologist together.

We have read books on relationships, sex addiction, and forgiveness. Today, we talk intimately, dance, and have good sex, but I don't think I am going to get over the betrayal. Though I have a great job, children who keep me busy, a grandchild, and good friends, I feel I am in limbo.

Our psychologist says we are both still healing. I am not sure why I wrote you. I suppose I would like to hear your opinion.

-Vanessa

Vanessa, your psychologist used the word "healing." Is that a metaphor or an accurate description of what is going on? About 20 years ago, Wayne fractured his clavicle. It was a bad break, and the x-ray showed wide separation between two parts of bone. In a few months the bone knitted together. Wayne never gives it a thought. Why? Because it healed.

What your psychologist calls healing sounds more like getting used to something distasteful. As a girl, you didn't dream your husband would be meeting men in public toilets for sex. That's like trying to get used to living in a prison: forget about the outside world, you're in here for life. Forget about your dreams and what you were raised to believe marriage is.

When we don't live from our authentic self, occasionally our true desires break through. Your desire was for an honest, faithful, loving husband. His desire is to be who he really is, when no one is looking.

When you prompted your husband to admit an addiction, you trapped yourself. If he has a disease, that makes you a bad person if you want to leave him.

Ask yourself if the latest round of counseling has simply gotten you more caught up in his story. To go to counseling with your husband is to let others alter your perceptions. You've read all the books and talked to the psychologists. Ten years ago, you were trying to decide whether to stay or go. Ten years later, you are still trying to decide.

-Wayne & Tamara

How do you understand the mind of a person who would do an act you wouldn't consider in your wildest dreams?

Many people who say they would immediately boot the cheater say that from a never-going-to-happen-to-me perspective. It's not as simple as they think. There will be far more consideration when it's actually you. When it is you, it's "but I have three kids and I'm a stay-at-home mom," or, "We own a business together."

Ethics are easy in the abstract. When in that moment you find out it is you, and not someone else, that is when you are vulnerable to the "we can make it even better" story or "it was only once, and I didn't care about her." That's when you are susceptible to "You have to take your part in this." That's when you are vulnerable to "Commit to a recovery process." Many people will advocate a course of action for you based on a belief rather than based on an honest, statistically reliable assessment of the risk. Framing the decision to stay as "saving marriages" or "being pro-marriage" puts a positive spin on it. But those terms are advertising slogans.

From the standpoint of risk, you are dealing with a known hazard whose life cycle is the length of your relationship. The only way to end the risk with that person is to end the relationship. You should hope it is not true that you can get past infidelity. If it is true, it means there are no stable relationships and no special connections.

If you stay, you may consider leaving when you have more proof, leaving when he confesses, leaving after we go to counseling for a week (or a month or a year), or leaving after we go to our minister or priest. If you stay, there is a possibility you will do a reverse cheat. You may not think you are capable of it, but this type of payback is common. Or you stay and start lying about your relationship to your friends and family, and your isolation increases. Or you have a blowup in front of the children.

Only one thing ends the possibility of another betrayal—leaving the relationship. If you end the relationship, you can figure out fairly accurately where you will stand. If you stay, there are too many unknowns to predict the results.

When you think about it, assessing risk is something we do all the time. We do it every time we cross a street, hire a babysitter, or decide the meat has been in the refrigerator too long. The key to understanding risk is to stop thinking in terms of what you want. Think in terms of what your situation is and accept that.

One U.S. company got in trouble for failing to tell customers it could reduce their credit line if they used their card at certain businesses.[1] The list of businesses included massage parlors, pawn shops, pool halls, tire retreading shops, and—marriage counselors. That is another way of looking at your relationship. If an insurance company assessed your risk, would they write you a policy? If so, how high would the premiums be?

Sometimes numbers win in deciding what to do. When a thing is overwhelmingly risky, you must go against your wants and desires. Now add in the factor that the other woman won't let go of him or works where he works. The percentages are constantly changing. It's not a matter of letting numbers trump love. When someone cheats on you, their love for your unique relationship is not there.

We take care of the things we love. That's proof cheaters don't love their partner. They didn't take care of them.

Sometimes you must pull your broken heart out of the mix and let the odds make the decision for you. Anyone who tells you how to manage this risk without walking you through a serious assessment of the hazards simply does not understand risk and risk management. They are steering you toward a foregone conclusion, which is the opposite of managing risk. They are preventing you from making an informed choice.

Some would prevent you from having a choice at all. If they urge you to commit to the marriage or go to a "pro-marriage" counselor, they are leading you to believe your marriage license enslaved you but not your partner.

It is hard for some people to accept the existence of a hazard because it conflicts with their value system. That explains why lay people refused to accept that some priests were pedophiles and many bishops and cardinals were covering it up.[2] It's why some parents silenced their own children who were victims of priestly sexual abuse. It all came to light not from internal reform but because of the actions of victims, journalists, and lawyers who forced church officials to reform. Reality conflicted with the congregants' belief system, and to preserve their belief system, they placed it above reality.

You can't do that.

Other betrayed people refuse to ACCEPT that their relationship is over because it threatens their identity.[3] They think the end of the relationship means:

- They have lost their 'place' in society.
- They have failed on a personal level.
- They have lost life itself.

If you are with an unfaithful partner and someone claiming expert knowledge urges you to stay or says, "You can get past this," they are exposing you to a hazard. Though they may feel they are doing the Lord's work, or what is expected of clinicians, or what is best for society, what they are not doing is assessing the amount of risk to you. Not wanting it to rain has nothing to do with whether it will rain.

It is a truism in the field of risk assessment that experts are *risk shifters*.[4] When what they say is incorrect or inaccurate, you, not they, suffer the consequences. In short, their status as expert enables them to stick out *your* neck.

When teachers construct a multiple-choice test, they include plausible distractors. A plausible distractor is not the right answer or the best answer, but it has some characteristic that will make people pick it as correct. Plausible distractors are attractive to the uninformed, and they take advantage of the uninformed.

One strategy used in constructing plausible distractors is to use concepts that resonate with people. They ring a bell. Some examples are forgiveness, closure, and the "sanctity of marriage." Scientific-sounding words can also be plausible distractors. But if you have been cheated on, your perceptions, uncolored by what others say, have given you the correct answer. Your body tells you the right answer.

Another plausible distractor is the 'duty' you owe to the relationship to stay. In this case, they are talking to the wrong party. Saying you have a duty to stay is an attempt to disguise the fact that the other person lied repeatedly by omission and commission and engaged in thousands of mental acts that you will never know about. Those acts include fantasizing about their lover, reliving moments with their lover, and planning how to get away from you to be with their lover.

Some people must run a gauntlet of plausible distractors before they can give themselves permission to end a relationship.

We don't think two people in love dance around each other. They dance with each other. If you have been betrayed, you can no longer think of you and your partner as "we." You are individual, and you have to act upon that. No quarter was given you when they did what they did. They gave themselves a reason to do it. They figured you wouldn't find out. This wasn't about fairness. It was about getting away with misconduct. It was about what they thought best for themselves.

Don't let anything other than reality affect the decision you make. If someone gets away with a crime, they are more likely to do it again.

Perhaps the only way a victim, especially a fresh victim of cheating, should go into counseling with an offending party is accompanied by someone who has their best interest at heart, perhaps their mom or dad, their brother or sister, or their best friend. They need someone who will act on their behalf. They need someone who won't be tricked into siding with the person who took advantage of them.

When you are in a state of shock, far from a position of clear thinking, you can't be thrown into an arena where two people gang up against you. Facts and knowledge are your friends. Simply reading this book, if you take away half a dozen ideas, will allow you to have a better understanding than someone who doesn't have this knowledge.

Knowledge makes us stronger. We must live in reality, not in "I wish," "I would like," or, "I would hope." It is not reality if it is not in your power to make it so. "I want him to be faithful" is not in your power to make happen. The person who cheated can do it again. Your existence did not stop them before. Your existence does not have the power to stop them again.

Many people can't think past "I'm hurt and don't want to break up." That's like saying, "I don't want to have cancer." It's not a choice. Cheating broke the promise, and the biopsy said it is cancer. The logical conclusion from the previous chapters is you should leave someone who cheats on you because you are not going to get over it. There is something odd in asking why he or she cheated. It implies their action is not normal, though it obviously is part of their character and part of their thinking process.

Essential Ingredient

I have a couple of questions for you. If a person no longer feels they love their spouse, is it time to divorce? Also, do you think a person who has had an affair can change enough for the betrayed to forgive and continue the marriage? Is it possible to salvage a marriage after the affair?

-Marie

164

Marie, a book could be written on each of your questions, but the last question sounds like the one you are really asking. What do you mean by salvage?

Do you mean the cake just fell on the floor and the guests are arriving? Can we patch it together and serve it from the kitchen so no one notices what happened? Or do you mean, after an affair, can you have the kind of marriage you would wish for your son or daughter?

Marriage is a relationship different from all others. You can date many people; you can be friends with many people; you can be neighbors to many people. But the act of getting married says, "I choose this one unique being to share everything with me for the rest of my life."

The basis for willingly binding yourself to one person is love. Their fidelity allows you to believe in their love. Their fidelity allows you to sustain your love. But if that person is unfaithful then they, not you, have brought their love into question. Infidelity validates your doubts about their love.

The idea of fidelity is in the marital vows because it is essential. Fidelity is the one thing promised in virtually every religious tradition and understood worldwide. Why? Because breaking faith breaks the marriage.

It is possible to forgive betrayal, but in our experience, it is not possible to forget it. That would be like forgetting you have kids. It isn't going to happen. The unfaithful person would like the other person to forget, and the one betrayed would like to forget, but barring amnesia they cannot.

How do you believe "I love you" after you have been betrayed? That is what people ask us years and even decades afterwards. For some people who stay in the marriage, divorce was not an option. For many people, it is not the case that they healed after infidelity. They simply live with the pain. Is that a marriage salvaged?

Others claim you can get over infidelity. We say you may not be able to overcome infidelity. The difference is we focus on the innocent party.

-Wayne & Tamara

We end this chapter with a column that asks the most basic question after betrayal.

As Hard as Stone

While working at a grocery store, I met a handsome guy. I fell in love the first time I saw him, happy in a way I never felt. He said he felt the same. We saw each other every day. He was in my mind night and day. I thought this much happiness was too good to be true. I gave so much I forgot to keep a little of me to myself.

Because of the past, I didn't want to mess this one up. I was so in love I didn't see the many red flags. I was blind and dumb. One day, we met at a park before I went to work. We talked and laughed about everything. He told me he had been separated from his ex-girlfriend for eight months. It was one of the best days of my life.

We moved in together, but right after the move I discovered he had been lying about so many things. It wasn't months ago he left his girlfriend. He was living with her after we started our relationship.

When I confronted him, he got mad and didn't answer my questions. I don't know why he lied to me. I don't know what I did to him. He would leave the house for days and then return and I would take him back. Why?

I don't know. I am so mad at myself for not having the courage, the self-respect, to leave him. Even when I felt my world tumbling down and realized he wasn't the guy I met, I didn't let go.

It is hard for me to understand how a person can say they love you, that you are the love of their life, yet lie and hurt you and leave without caring. I never got answers to my questions and I was devastated.

Can I be the person I was before? Did I do something wrong to deserve this?

-Abbey

Abbey, we don't deserve the rain. We don't deserve the accidents that happen. We can't look at what others do as our fault. As you are free to be a good person, so are they free to decide what kind of person they will be.

There is no reason you shouldn't be the person you were before him because this is not your fault. But you have learned something. The first time someone treats you like this—lies, disrespects, leaves—don't take them back. Skip the "repeatedly took him back" step and just move on.

Just as what he did is not your fault, you must accept that you cannot change who he is. Only he can do that, and he doesn't find fault in his behavior. So he will not change.

That's the trap many women need to let go of. "It's me," and, "He'll change." What does "it's me" mean? It means "How did I cause him to be like this?" You didn't. It's not you. You didn't make him who he is.

People can't change who they are in their base nature. They form as they grow up. Who they are is more permanent than a tattoo. Thinking they can change themselves for you weds you to an impossible goal.

Trying to be someone you are not, trying to get someone to be who they are not, is a lifetime of pushing a boulder up a hill. Today you have to do it; tomorrow you have to do it; next year you have to do it.

In the beginning people trick themselves into thinking they can push the rock because they have just started pushing. But after months and years all they can think is, "Why am I pushing this rock?" That's the trap. To have what they want today, they start something they cannot sustain.

-Wayne & Tamara

Abbey asked, "Can I be the person I was before?" That's one way to phrase the topic of the next chapter. That chapter is called Recover.

CHAPTER 18
RECOVER

"Whatever must happen ultimately should happen immediately."

—Henry Kissinger, diplomat

Dear Wayne and Tamara,

Can you start me on the road to recovery and renewal?

During the past few years I have had a background feeling something was missing from my life or I was travelling in the wrong direction. I have never been able to get to the bottom of the question "What do I want to be when I grow up?"

I am now nearly 49, have been married for nearly 30 years, and our partnership has weathered storms, and we have shared good and bad times. We have moved quite frequently, now in our 13th (?) house and 4th country. I have gathered friends in several places, some of whom I try to visit and correspond with regularly.

Four years ago, my husband moved to Greece for his employment, which was intended to be a short-term placement. As my youngest son was still in school, I stayed in England. Last year, that son and I came to join my husband. My employers agreed to my proposal of distance working for possibly two years. Initially, I had an office within my husband's company building. Ten months ago, I started working from home.

One of my husband's female colleagues shared our house until she was re-located a month or so ago. She was my only companion. I took language lessons for a while but had little opportunity to meet with like-minded people as the expat crowd gathered together during the day while I was working. Now I only leave the house once or twice a week and have only the companionship of my husband and, occasionally, his friends.

All of these circumstances culminated in me feeling dissatisfied, unhappy, demotivated, and unsure how to shape my future.

My husband has friends and acquaintances gained through work and interest pursuits, many of whom have come to the house from time to time. Recently, one of his contractors asked for his help with a business proposal, so she came to the house more frequently and they also met elsewhere.

After a meeting at our house behind closed doors, I was 'summoned' to join them. I was advised that they had a close and deep friendship they would like to continue, with my consent, but it was strictly a friendship and not a sexual relationship. I felt humiliated to be consulted in that way.

In the past we have weathered his affairs and passing flirtations but, probably due to my low level of happiness at this time, this situation is very painful for me. My husband and I have had a number of emotional conversations, which, previously, I have not been able to do—so that is one positive outcome.

I think, through these discussions, I realize I have been dissatisfied with our relationship for a long time. I told him that I want to change its basis. We have no leisure pursuits in common, we do not holiday together, and recently he advised I should get some friends of my own. I am now endeavoring to join some interest groups.

We are both willing to make efforts towards establishing a more satisfying relationship, but I just don't know where to start. When my husband goes to visit his close female friend, he does not get home until four or five in the morning and I am unable to sleep. I don't know whether I am jealous or envious that they have more in common. Is this a real problem or just a focus for all the other things that are wrong in my life? How do I start the rebuild?

-Carissa

170

Carissa raises a good question, though we would rephrase it this way: What does it take for you to look forward to the rest of your life?

Neuroscientist and student of creativity Tina Seelig reports that 70% of all people suffer or will suffer from Imposter Syndrome.[1] Imposter Syndrome makes people feel that other people are more grown up and capable than they are. As an example, Tina uses Stanford University, where she teaches. When new business students are asked if they feel they are the one mistake the admissions department made, two-thirds of these talented people raise their hand.

Imposter Syndrome is an equal opportunity insecurity. It affects people from all backgrounds. Seelig suggests instead of seeing yourself as unworthy, examine your life and realize you are living only one of the possible lives you might live.

In *Designing Your Life,* Bill Burnett and Dave Evans describe life as the process of designing something that never existed before.[2] Most of us aren't born with a passion, we discover it only through experience and reflection, and Burnett and Evans start from a simple premise. You must begin from where you are right now. Take a look at your life as if looking at the dashboard of a car. Check the gauges, especially the ones that measure health, work, play, and love.

In *Designing Your Life,* Burnett and Evans demonstrate how to take your interests, values, and what you care about and turn that knowledge into three completely different lives you could have in the next five years. These lives are not A, B, and C, with A being the first choice. No, they are three separate life plans, each an A in its own right.

A book with a more personal focus is *Designing the Life You Love* by Ayse Birsel.[3] In the beginning of her book, Birsel asks for 20 minutes of your time. She wants you to consider everything in your life: hobbies, habits, values, rituals, friendships, work, strengths, joys, goals, and health. Then she demonstrates how to take your life apart, see it differently, and put it back together the way you want.

Birsel's exercises, like those of Burnett and Evans, yield insights into your life you may not be able to reach in any other way. They can help you move from my life today to "My life as I want it." These are only two of the good books in this genre. Explore them.

Some people are not ready for a life redesign. They are stuck at an earlier stage of recovery. These people may fit into the first two of what Glenn Schiraldi calls the three different mindsets after trauma.[4] The three mindsets are victim, survivor, and thriver. Victims feel helpless and passive, numb or defeated. Survivors are beginning to take control and know the pain is starting to lessen. Thrivers are resilient and strong. Life is under their control. They are happy from day to day and plan for the future.

If you are caught in victim or survivor mode, individual counseling with someone who understands trauma may be the most helpful thing you can do.[5] We offer this advice with only one caveat. Find someone good.

Not all counselors are equal. We cannot imply that "go to counseling" is completely safe advice. We have received letters from people who cheated with their marriage counselor. One man and his mistress went into counseling to learn how to get along. The man's wife, of course, knew nothing about this form of "couples counseling".

In the first year of our column, a Canadian man told us his wife slept with her psychotherapist, a man who promised her a trip to France and a business opportunity if she left her husband. Another man suspected his wife was involved with their minister. After this extramarital activity was exposed, the minister received a sudden "calling from God" to minister to souls on a Pacific island 7,300 air miles away. The minister and his family promptly moved there.

However, the most common complaint we receive about therapy is it is ineffective. Yet we still recommend individual counseling for two reasons. First, people wounded by betrayal often cannot find their way out without professional help, and second, some people report their individual counseling was life changing.

Betrayal is hard to get out of your mind. The longer the relationship, the more memories a person is tied to. That's why it's helpful to find things that harness your energy in another direction. Career strategist Jenny Blake recommends cultivating a hobby or skill that can fully occupy your mind while engaging your body. Blake herself coped with the challenge of career changes by learning to do handstands during yoga class.[6]

Most of us aren't interested in handstands, but Blake's advice is valid. As she says, hobbies get you out of your head. Time off from pressing worries lets you see things in a new way and developing a skill builds confidence. It rewires the brain. It can teach you how to overcome challenges.

An activity that might appeal to some people is shadow dancing. Shadow dancing, as Jim Joseph describes it, is solo dancing in private. Holding your arms up in the closed ballroom position, perhaps in a darkened room, imagine yourself with a partner. Then find the beat in the music, learn a new dance step, and burn the rhythm pattern into your mind.[7]

Guitars and keyboards are cheap. If the idea appeals to you, find a teacher on the internet and learn to play an instrument. That will take all your attention and focus. Learning an art or a craft can also help. As one woman told us, "For me, clay, a music keyboard, and a ukulele are all new the last year, and I've been surprised at how therapeutic they are. They align my brain cells...Who'd have thought?"

When Tamara was battling breast cancer, she began playing a survival video game called *The Long Dark*. Previously she had no interest in video games, but she found this one game, set in the Canadian wilderness, a great way to forget about the life-and-death issues she was facing. She often caught herself leaning right or left as she peered around a corner or jumping back when startled by a wolf or bear.

Picking a hobby, skill, or project that appeals to you can help you recover. Importantly, the activity should completely occupy your mind, engage your body, and take significant amounts of time to master. It should be immersive. The point of the activity is not to hide from life but to gain a few hours of relief from the problems you face.

As a final point on recovery, let us mention a suggestion from productivity expert David Allen, the author of *Getting Things Done*. For each aspect of your life, Allen recommends asking, "What is the next physical, observable action I might do to move it forward?"[8] If you want to redesign your life, what next visible action-step will move the process along? Do it. Then do the action-step after that, and so on.

Always thinking in terms of the next action step is one of the most powerful ways to change your life because, unfortunately, research indicates people are biased in favor of staying put.[9] When given a situation with different options, most people do nothing. They 'vote' for the status quo. Not because it is the best option, but because, we would say, it is the option that allows them to avoid a decision.

You cannot change if you are unwilling to change. Change means disconnecting from your past. Disconnecting is the topic of the next chapter.

CHAPTER 19
DISCONNECT

"No one's soul moves alone, Leweth. When one love dies, one must learn to love another."

—R. Scott Bakker, fantasy author

After 25 years of marriage, I found out my husband was cheating on me with an employee at our company. I was overwhelmed with fear, hurt beyond words and confused as to what to do next.

I sought out a counselor who offered me hope and encouragement that this could all be worked out in time. I also searched the internet trying to figure out what other women had done in my situation. But to say my world had been turned upside down would be an understatement.

During that search I came across your website and an article I believe changed the course of my life. Under a section called "Getting Past Cheating" there was a letter from someone named Marie.

She asked many questions and ended with, "...do you think a person who has had an affair can change enough for the betrayed to forgive and continue the marriage? Is it possible to salvage a marriage after the affair?"

You said, "Marie, a book could be written on each of your questions, but the last question sounds like the one you are really asking. What do you mean by salvage? Do you mean the cake just fell on the floor and the guests are arriving? Can we patch it up and serve it from the kitchen so no one notices what happened?

"Or do you mean, after an affair, can you have the kind of marriage you would wish for your son or daughter?"

I read the article and it resonated because it was the first one that said maybe every marriage isn't worth saving after all. And no, I remember thinking I wouldn't want this for my son or anyone else I loved. So I put a copy of it on my computer desktop and stuck a copy in my wallet.

In between, there were all the voices telling me if I could just tough it out and try to put it behind me, then maybe, just maybe, I might have some 'shadow' of a marriage. But I would take your article out and read it over and over.

I ran across an infidelity survival website, and I remember a woman who said she was "back again" because having made it through eight years of reconciliation hell, she just found out her husband was cheating again. That made me think back to what you had written and it stopped me in my tracks again.

Eventually, I found a second counselor who gently but firmly helped me accept that my husband had Narcissistic Personality Disorder (NPD). With time, I was able to begin to understand I had been in an emotionally abusive relationship all along.

That insight came way down the road and led me to file for divorce. You can probably imagine what divorcing an abusive man with NPD was like, but I stood my ground and it worked out for me in the end. When I finally reached the point where being homeless was better than staying, I knew however it ended it would be OK.

So here I am nearly three years since this all happened, and I've never been so happy. Last year, I moved into my own condo, and although it's not big and fancy like my old home, it's my home. And when on the first night in my new place I found myself sitting on my porch, sipping a cup of coffee and looking up at a sky full of stars, I finally knew peace.

Still, even today, I pull your article out of my wallet and read it again just to remind myself how far I've come and how grateful I am that I stumbled across it. So thank you from the bottom of my heart for your wisdom and being willing to be honest.

-Noel

Another woman wrote, "Tell me what you think of this."

My husband cheated on me for maybe five years, and yes, I really had no idea. The person he cheated with is a policewoman on his job; she is married and her husband is a cop. So to make a long story short, I found out about the affair and forgave him, but a few years later I realized it was still ongoing.

Out of anger I called her husband and told him, plus I gave him a lot of damaging proof. I then filed a complaint with her captain to keep her from calling my house. Now my husband is trying to save his good name with the department and avoiding contact with her husband. As for me, my husband is playing the "forgive me" role again, but this time I'm letting him believe things are okay.

I'm back at school full-time for my degree, I turn nothing down he offers, and I ask for everything. Most of the time I get it. I'm going places I only dreamed about, and I'm enjoying it for me! Not for us. I am determined to be a better independent me, able to take care of myself. What he does for me, even if it's out of guilt, hey, I deserve it and more. I am going to take it all, and, in the end, he will know what it is like to put your trust and belief in one person only to have them change their mind and walk out with no regrets.

This I am going to do, 'cause it's all about me now. I forgot one more thing; I have been faithfully married to this man for over twenty years.

-Vivian

A man writes:

Wayne and Tamara, I hope you can help me with a situation I find unbearable. I recently discovered that my wife had an affair last year. During the time when she had the affair her behavior was completely out of the ordinary. She was cold and distant and refused to have sex for almost six months. I begged her to go to counseling, but she refused and would not discuss it.

I suspected something at the time, but she has always been EXTREMELY adamant that cheating is wrong, and I've heard her on many occasions say how terrible someone was for doing it. I was convinced that she would never cheat on me. I should also point out that we have never had a very good marriage. There have always been arguments and problems, but I never resorted to cheating.

I have two boys 10 and 11 years old and I love them more than anything in the world. I would like to divorce her, but she would surely get physical custody of the children and I couldn't live without seeing them every day—they are the most important thing to me.

I feel trapped because she betrayed me, and the kids and I have to pay for it. I am left with two choices, live in an unbearable circumstance with her or divorce and leave my kids. It's not fair, I resent it, and it's tearing me apart.

-Mike

Maltreatment, in some instances, strengthens the bond between two people. Some people feel any relationship is better than none. "At least I'm not alone. I can ignore the evidence, believe they will not do it again, and accept my fate." Feeling like that, however, doesn't negate reality. As trauma expert Jasmine Cori says, if someone you know and especially someone you love is the source of the trauma, it leaves the worst scars.[1]

But don't blame the other man or woman. There are millions of women and men out there. None of them made a promise to you. Only one person did: your husband or wife, your boyfriend or girlfriend, your partner. Apologists for cheating may pile excuse upon excuse, but the question remains, are you with someone who is faithful or not? Cheating apologists may try to make the essence of the act disappear, but the question is simple. Did the magician really make the dove disappear or is it still there, concealed?

The few letters we receive from people who stayed and claim success fall into two categories. The first category is "We have established a tit-for-tat relationship, with boundaries and agreements, terms and conditions." That's not love.[2] The second category of letters says go to this website or read this book. These writers want to believe that, somewhere out there, there must be an answer to how to get past cheating.

We have never received a letter that read, "I healed. I never think about it."

Death of a Marriage

On Friday I will be moving out of my large four-bedroom, two-bath, two-car garage home. I will not see my kids every day, and I believe this is the end of my 12-year marriage. I keep hoping moving out will restart our relationship.

The cause of the move is my wife's rediscovery of my cheating. The first time happened after I infected her with trichomoniasis. We both cried and were hurt. She promised to forgive me, and I promised never to cheat again. I also agreed not to look at online pornography. I understood looking at porn or cheating again would mean the end of the marriage.

I failed. It wasn't because I didn't love her. I think it was an addiction to sex and taking my wife for granted. My viewing of internet porn started a month after my wife agreed to make the marriage work, and this led me on a downward spiral.

I can't explain it, but going back to the prostitute again was a form of closure for me. I needed to dominate the woman who started everything to unravel. The act was pleasurable, and she was more animated than my wife. I left feeling vindicated and that I never had to return.

My movements became more secretive. Last Tuesday, I looked at internet porn at work, wrote down numbers of some ladies, and planned to call and get pricing. I kept telling myself I just wanted to hear their voices, but I was collecting them. I put the paper in my shirt pocket to call them on the commute home.

I was going to dispose of the paper before I got home, and no one would be the wiser. Well, I forgot, and my wife discovered the paper. She told me to move out by Friday. I didn't argue. I started packing and sent a quick email to the pastor who counsels us.

My fear is there will be no way to make up with my wife. I continue to ask for another chance, but her heart is cold to me. She says I can come over for dinner and have the kids stay at my new place, but I don't know how to win her back.

-Tim

Tim, some things, like electricity, are hard to understand. Even though we use electricity every day, most of us cannot say what it is. Nonetheless, it follows basic laws, and if we violate its laws, electricity can kill us. In the same way, there are basic behavioral laws, and if we fail to follow them, they will kill a relationship.

No one would suggest you get to live in a house you cannot pay for, receive a paycheck you didn't work for, or get a perfect score on a test you didn't study for. Why do you think you get to keep the wife you were unfaithful to? What has happened follows behavioral laws, which are almost as predictable as the laws of electricity.

You brought home a sexually transmitted disease, but you could just as easily have created a half-brother or half-sister for your children. You got to experience adultery and moments of pleasure, and now you get to experience separation, divorce, and perhaps making payments on a house you don't get to live in.

Everything that happened is based on what you decided to do, but you can't say that about your wife. You will end up divorced because of what you did, but she will end up divorced because of what somebody did to her. She was in a real marriage, the marriage of "we." You were in a false marriage, the marriage of "I."

An ancient Chinese maxim says if you are out for vengeance, dig two graves. The same might be said of your infidelity. Your infidelity dug one grave for you and another for her.

-Wayne & Tamara

Even if you don't disconnect from a cheater, knowing what you would do if you left will help. Uncertainty leaves you hanging. Planning life without them will partially ease your reluctance to face your fears.

CHAPTER 20
CONCLUSION

"If you want a happy ending, that depends, of course, on where you stop your story."

—Orson Welles, actor and writer

Thomas More, Henry VIII's lord chancellor, was so principled a man that Catholics consider him a saint. More coined the word utopia, a name he gave to his vision of an ideal society. In his book *Utopia*, divorce was permitted both for couples who couldn't get along and for adultery. In the case of adultery, the couple was legally divorced and the innocent party free to remarry, but the adulterer or adulteress was condemned to slavery.

If the innocent partner could not shake off their love for the offending partner, however, they were allowed to accompany the offender into slavery.[1] Perhaps More was saying that remaining with your betrayer is enslavement. If you stay, you will be in continual psychological torment and bondage.

Our minds are not a blank slate. We are not free to overwrite certain programs in our mind. One of these programs is a cheater detection program. It refuses to accept the treachery and duplicity of a cheater. It constantly sounds an alarm in their presence. Other programs we know as the emotions. A particular group of emotions occurs within victims of a cheater. These two different programs are automatic, inbuilt, and beyond conscious control. They are embedded in the architecture of the human person.

183

If you were cheated upon, you are drowning in a maelstrom of feelings. We wrote this book to help you see the order within that turmoil and to find a way out. We know that, if you just discovered your partner is having an affair, the one thing you can't do well is reason clearly. We also know that staying with a cheater requires you to collapse your normal defenses, a task which is nearly impossible.

A scientific model is a representation of something that occurs in the real world. A good model clarifies thinking. It makes features of the world easier to understand. Even though scientific models are abstractions, they represent the essential elements of what they describe. Models are true to the extent they fit current facts and to the extent they can be used to predict events in the future. A valid model need not predict every case, but it should predict typical cases.

That's what this book is. It is a model of what occurs in a person betrayed. We didn't take our model from any other source. Indeed, we have never seen it anywhere else. It comes directly from letters written to us by people who have been betrayed.

We wrote this book to help those people understand the structure of their experience. We summarized that structure with the acronym DAST. DAST is a model that captures the archetypal reactions to a cheater: disgust, anger, suspicion, and trauma. Disgust is the opposite of love; its central feature is revulsion. Anger is the emotion that protects us from the injustice of betrayal. Suspicion is our natural reaction toward those we cannot trust. Trauma is a general bodily upset.

Whether you believe our bodies were fashioned by millions of years of evolution or fashioned in the image and likeness of God, or some combination of the two, it does not matter. When you feel disgust, anger, and suspicion—and your body and brain go into a high alarm that won't quit—your body and mind are reacting exactly as they should to the continued presence of a cheater. You may be miserable, but your mind and body are reacting exactly as they were designed to react.

In the previous three chapters, we suggested a way out for victims of cheating. We now summarize that way out with the acronym ARD. The "A" stands for accept. You can't find your way out of this problem, or any problem, without first accepting your situation. The "R" stands for recover. Recovery means reimagining your life. For those most damaged, recovery may require professional help through individual counseling. The "D" stands for disconnect. In the letters we receive, those who disconnect from the cheater are most capable of finding a good life.

We are not trying to be cute, but if you put the two acronyms together, they spell a word. The word is *dastard*. A dastard is someone who commits an underhanded or treacherous act. There is no way to finesse this. Cheating is an underhanded, treacherous act. That is its nature. Each of us seeks the one for us. That's what cheating destroys, the idea that our partner chose us alone.

Why did we take the time to write a book saying cheating is bad? Because some people write books saying it is no big deal or if it is a big deal, you can get past it. If you heard this, it might have slid over your head, like white noise. Without thinking, you may have thought, *That makes sense.* Or you may have questioned it a bit but thought the people who say this look like normal people. They're on TV. The word "expert" is in their biography. *They must be right. I must not know enough to understand what they are talking about.* That's what you may have thought.

We also wrote this book to give justice to victims of betrayal. We find much of the advice on staying with a cheater repugnant. Some of it, when offered by psychologists or therapists, we find ethically questionable. Some of it, when offered by clergy, we find lacking in a genuine sense of morality. One of the oddest things about forgiveness literature is that it gives an escape to the bad party and punishes the good party. Some writers allow a cheater to cry, "Sanctuary!" and be protected while the victim of cheating is not protected. These writers act as if "saving marriages" is one of the Ten Commandments. It isn't. However, not committing adultery and not considering adultery are two of the ten.

Some people will make excuses for your mate, as if he or she is simply confused about priorities, values, goals, and needs. But they are not confused about how to drive a car, what a stop sign means, and how to mail a letter. They know how to put on a pair of pants. They know not to leave a restaurant without paying. If they do leave without paying, what is their defense? "I didn't know I was supposed to pay?"

We didn't start with an axe to grind.

We didn't care if the answer is stay after someone cheats on you or leave if someone cheats on you. We are free to look at the facts of human life and free to examine the reasoning of those who take a position. We are not hemmed in by a religious belief that requires us to defend one position or the other. We are not stuck on a therapeutic model that chokes our view of the world. We cared only about finding the right answer.

In this book, we give you the answer we found.

As we said in the preface, our aim is to give you a book that fits the reality of betrayal. You can act on it or not, as you choose. Perhaps, because it offers a path you don't want to consider, you will reject the path for now. We believe at some point you will come back to it because it represents the underlying pattern of human experience.

In the end, only you can make the decision. Only you will suffer the consequences or reap the benefits of what you do.

We began the book by quoting Dick Young, a character in a novel by Daphne du Maurier. Dick said, "Truth is the hardest thing to put across." We agree, and we would define truth as that which corresponds to facts. Truth is not what we wish to be true or what we would hope to be true. Truth is what corresponds to facts.

Thousands of people wrote us. They had a story to tell. This book is the explanation of that story.

Author Website:
WayneAndTamara.com

NOTES

Names of letter writers have been changed. Some letters were edited for style, brevity, or to conform to U.S. English spelling and usage.

Preface
1. Daphne du Maurier. *The House on the Strand*, 285.

Chapter 1 Your World Overturned
Maurizio Viroli. *Niccolo's Smile: A Biography of Machiavelli*, 131.

1. Laura Betzig. "Causes of Conjugal Dissolution: A Cross-cultural Study."

2. The verses are Matthew 1:19-20 and Matthew 5:32. The interpretation among Christian groups is contentious.

3. Israel Charny and S. Parnass. "The Impact of Extramarital Relationships on the Continuation of Marriages."

4. James Twitchell. *Twenty Ads That Shook the World*, 88-101.

5. Barbara Dafoe Whitehead and David Popenoe. "Who Wants to Marry a Soul Mate?" 6, 8. Barbara Dafoe Whitehead and David Popenoe. "Singles Seek Soul Mates for Marriage."

6. Mark M. Gray, Paul M. Perl, and Tricia C. Bruce. "Marriage in the Catholic Church." PDF

7. Lynn A. Baker and Robert E. Emery. "When Every Relationship Is Above Average."

Results among young adults seem to be consistent. In 2012 psychologist Jeffrey Jensen Arnett conducted a nationwide poll and reported that 86% of 18- to 29-year-olds surveyed expect to have a marriage that will last a lifetime. Arnett said, "It is striking to see how optimistic today's emerging adults are about their prospects for having a life-long marriage. They grow up knowing that half of marriages end in divorce, yet nearly all of them expect to be in the half that doesn't." Jeffrey Jensen Arnett and Joseph Schwab. "The Clark University Poll of Emerging Adults."

Chapter 2 Disgust

C.S. Lewis. *Till We Have Faces: A Myth Retold*, 177. The exact quote is: "You grow more and more a stranger to me at each word. And I had loved you so; loved, honoured, trusted, and (while it was fit) obeyed."

1. Paul Ekman. *Emotions Revealed: Recognizing Faces and Feelings to Improve Communication and Emotional Life*, 2-3.

2. For a brief summary, see: Judy Foreman. "A Conversation With: Paul Ekman." New York Times, 5 Aug 2003. Ekman initially thought there were six basic emotions, then expanded his list to seven.

3. Ekman, 14.

4. Ibid., 18-20.

5. A pioneer in the study of how neural circuitry helps organize the emotions was Jaak Panksepp, author of *Affective Neuroscience: The Foundations of Human and Animal Emotion*.

6. For example, Robert Plutchik viewed emotions as behavioral solutions to the universal problems of life. Robert Plutchik. "A General Psychoevolutionary Theory of Emotion." 3-33.

7. Jesse J. Prinz. *Gut Reactions: A Perceptual Theory of Emotion*, 89-90.

8. Words in different languages often don't overlap in meaning. One attempt to correct for this is the GRID project at the Center for Affective Sciences, University of Geneva.

9. Ekman, 27-28.

10. Ibid., 67.

11. Paul Rozin, Jonathan Haidt, and Clark R. McCauley. In *Handbook of Emotions*.

12. Ibid., 771.

13. William Ian Miller. *The Anatomy of Disgust*.

14. Ibid., 2.

15. Ibid., 86.

16. Ibid., xi, 50, 64-66.

17. Ibid., 66.

18. Ibid., 33.

19. Therapist Ben Caldwell says even the American Association for Marriage and Family Therapy can't agree whether it's couple therapy, couple's therapy, or couples therapy. A recent issue of its magazine used all three terms within the first seven pages. Psychotherapy Notes (blog).

20. Paul Rozin and April Fallon. *What Is America Eating?*, 68.

Chapter 3 – Anger
Loretta Lynn. Often quoted, original source unknown.

1. Aristotle. *Nicomachean Ethics*, Book 2.6.

2. Ibid., Book 4.5.

3. Ibid., Book 2.6.

4. Ibid., Book 5.2.

5. Sarah F. Brosnan and Frans B. M. de Waal. "Monkeys Reject Unequal Pay." Frans de Waal. *Our Inner Ape*, 207-209.

6. Frans de Waal. *Good Natured: the origins of right and wrong in humans and other animals,* 166-167. de Waal, *Our Inner Ape,* 210-214.

7. Golnaz Tabibnia, Ajay B. Satpute, and Matthew D. Lieberman. "The Sunny Side of Fairness: Preference for fairness activates reward circuitry (and disregarding unfairness activates self-control circuitry)."

8. *The Artist's Way,* 61. "Anger is our friend…a very, very loyal friend. It will always tell us when we have been betrayed." 62.

Chapter 4 – Suspicion
Friedrich Nietzsche. *Beyond Good and Evil,* Part IV, aphorism 183.

1. Myron Rothbart and Bernadette Park. "On the Confirmability and Disconfirmability of Trait Concepts."

2. Paul Slovic. "Perceived Risk, Trust and Democracy," 319-323. Slovic quotes Abraham Lincoln: "If you *once* forfeit the confidence of your fellow citizens, you can *never* regain their respect and esteem." 319. (Slovic's emphasis)

3. Leda Cosmides and John Tooby. "Evolutionary Psychology: A Primer."

4. Leda Cosmides and John Tooby. "Social Exchange: The Evolutionary Design of a Neurocognitive System." 1295-1308. This article describes Wasson selection tasks as logical and as social problems, with corresponding results. The "Ebbinghaus Disease Problem" is an example of an abstract logical problem most people struggle with. 1298.

5. Leda Cosmides, H. Clark Garrett, and John Tooby. "Adaptive Specializations, Social Exchange, and the Evolution of Human Intelligence."

6. Cosmides (2005)

7. Dan Zak. "The Truth About Lying." Washington Post, 25 Nov 2007.

8. P.L. 92-603.

Chapter 5 – Trauma

1. Stephen Porter and Kristine A. Peace. "The Scars of Memory: A prospective, longitudinal investigation of the consistency of traumatic and positive emotional memories in adulthood."

Compare to: "The current evidence from systematic and methodologically sound studies strongly suggests that memories of traumatic events are more resistant to forgetting than memories of mundane events..." Svein Magnussen and Annika Melinder. "What Psychologists Know and Believe about Memory: A Survey of Practitioners." (see Discussion)

2. Glenn R. Schiraldi. *The Post-Traumatic Stress Disorder Sourcebook: A Guide to Healing, Recovery, and Growth.* 2nd ed., 5, fig 1.1, 8.

3. Babette Rothschild. *8 Keys to Safe Trauma Recovery: Take-Charge Strategies to Empower Your Healing,* 77-78.

4. Dominic Gates. "20 Years Ago, Pilot's Heroic Efforts Saved 185 People As Plane Crashed." *Seattle Times,* 19 Jul 2009.

Jacob Gershman (as told to). "Crash Diary No. 2." In Al Haynes words, "My job had been to get people from point A to point B safely, and I didn't do it. I felt that I had killed them."

5. Joe Godfrey. "Al Haynes."

6. Howard Berkes. "Hero Pilot in 1989 United Crash Dies." NPR 10 May 2012. Comment from Veronica Gutierrez: "My uncle died in this crash. These gentlemen were amazing in their efforts. My aunt visited Al Haynes in his hospital bed to thank him for doing everything he could." https://www.npr.org/blogs/thetwo-way/2012/05/10/152402632/hero-pilot-in-1989-united-crash-dies (NPR deleted the Two-Way in 2018.)

7. Ann Carnahan. "Beyond Survival: Life's trials continued for pilot after 1989 crash (Al Haynes United Flight 232)." Rocky Mountain News, 7 May 2005.

The quote is from: Al Haynes. "The Crash of United Flight 232 by Capt. Al Haynes."

8. Linda L. Carli. "Cognitive Reconstruction, Hindsight, and Reactions to Victims and Perpetrators."

9. "The CAPS is widely considered to be the 'gold standard' in PTSD assessment." International Society for Traumatic Stress Studies.

"The CAPS is the gold standard in PTSD assessment." U.S. Veterans Administration.

10. A fourth area, cognition and moods symptoms, has more recently been added.

A study to define the core symptoms of PTSD is: Jessica L. Walton et al. "Sometimes Less is More: Establishing the core symptoms of PTSD."

11. The trauma recovery process has been analyzed in countless ways.

The oldest framework of trauma recovery is 3-phase scheme developed by Pierre Janet in the late 1800s. Medical doctor Judith Herman used this commonsense scheme in her classic work *Trauma and Recovery* (1992). The three phases are safety and stabilization, remembrance and processing, and integration of the experience into a fulfilling life. A concise description of the three phases is: "Phases of Trauma Recovery." Manitoba Trauma Information & Education Centre. trauma-recovery.ca/recovery/phases-of-trauma-recovery/ (retrieved 11 June 2019)

The view presented here is the 4-step model for recovery from primary and secondary traumatic stress. The four steps are the traumatic event, a period of safety, attempts to integrate the traumatic event, followed by success or chronic victimization. See Chrys J. Harris. "Sensory-based Therapy for Crisis Counselors." 103-105.

Rose Zimering and Suzy Bird Gulliver remark, "The vivid recounting of trauma by the survivor and the clinician's subsequent cognitive or emotional representation of that event may result in a set of symptoms and reactions that parallel PTSD (e.g., re-experiencing, avoidance and hyperarousal)." "Secondary Traumatization in Mental Health Care Providers."

12. Rothschild, 48-49.

Chapter 6 – The Emotions

Jesse Prinz. *Gut Reactions: A Perceptual Theory of Emotion.* 240.

1. Ekman, 2-14.

2. Cosmides (1997).

3. Jonathan Haidt. "The Emotional Dog and its Rational Tail: A social intuitionist approach to moral judgment." The full quote is "The time may be right, therefore, to take another look at Hume's perverse thesis: that moral emotions and intuitions drive moral reasoning, just as surely as a dog wags its tail."

In *Descartes' Error*, neurologist Antonio Damasio describes a man whose brain surgery deprived him of emotion. Though the patient could reason clearly, he no longer cared about the results; as a result, he made one disastrous decision after another.

Damasio concluded the man's defects emerged at the last stage of reasoning, where emotional values enable us to make the correct choice. Antonio R. Damasio. *Descartes' Error: Emotion, Reason, and the Human Brain.* 34-51.

4. Alan Watkins. *Coherence: The Secret Science of Brilliant Leadership.* 118-121.

5. David Watson. *Mood and Temperament.* 3-4.

Chapter 7 – Risk

Nassim Nicholas Taleb. *The Black Swan: The Impact of the Highly Improbable.* 133.

1. Of the eight statements in the problem, only two are relevant for our purposes. Amos Tversky and Daniel Kahneman. "Judgments of and by Representativeness." 84-98. Also Daniel Kahneman and Shane Frederick. "Representativeness Revisited: Attribute Substitution in Intuitive Judgment." 62.

2. Amos Tversky and Derek J. Koehler. "Support Theory: A Nonextensional Representation of Subjective Probability."

3. Amos Tversky and Daniel Kahneman. "Extensional versus Intuitive Reasoning: The conjunction fallacy in probability judgment." 37-38.

4. Roger C. Schank. *Tell Me a Story: Narrative and Intelligence (Rethinking Theory)*. 5-6.

5. Glynis M. Breakwell. *The Psychology of Risk*. 94-95.

6. This discussion of risk, hazard, and harm follows Breakwell, 1-2.

7. Ali Siddiq Alhakami and Paul Slovic. "A Psychological Study of the Inverse Relationship Between Perceived Risk and Perceived Benefit."

8. People lie to present a better version of themselves, because they misperceive themselves, and to please survey takers. For example, in one survey, 40% of people in the U.S. said they go to church every Sunday. The actual figure is 22%. C. Kirk Hadaway and Penny Long Marler. "How Many Americans Attend Worship Each Week? An Alternative Approach to Measurement."

Seth Stephens-Davidowitz demonstrated how internet search results tell a different from survey results. *Everybody Lies: Big Data, New Data, and What the Internet Can Tell Us About Who We Really Are.*

9. In fact, it's even the title of a paper. Michael Conway and Michael Ross. "Getting what you want by revising what you had."

10. David A. Armor and Shelley E. Taylor. "When Predictions Fail: The Dilemma of Unrealistic Optimism." 344.

11. David Dunning, Judith A. Meyerowitz, and Amy D. Holzberg. "Ambiguity and Self-Evaluation: The Role of Idiosyncratic Trait Definitions in Self-Serving Assessments of Ability." 324-333.

12. Kayla Knopp et al. "Once a Cheater, Always a Cheater? Serial Infidelity Across Subsequent Relationships."

13. This is optimistic bias. See Armor and Taylor above.

14. Timothy D. Wilson, David B. Centerbar, and Nancy Brekke. "Mental Contamination and the Debiasing Problem." 195.

Chapter 8 – Lying

Roger C. Schank. *Tell Me a Story: Narrative and Intelligence (Rethinking Theory)*. 209.

1. Ibid., 7.

2. Elizabeth Edwards. *Resilience: Reflections on the Burdens and Gifts of Facing Life's Adversities*. See the edition "with a powerful new afterword."

3. Neil A. Lewis. "For Edwards, Drama Builds Toward a Denouement." New York Times, 20 Sep 2009. John Edwards account of the affair can be found in "Transcript: John Edwards Interview: Read selections of Bob Woodruff's Interview With John Edwards." In this interview he still denies fathering a child with Rielle Hunter.

4. Sissela Bok. *Lying: Moral Choice in Public and Private Life*. 8, 13.

5. Adapted from J. J. Luna. *How to Be Invisible: Protect Your Home, Your Children, Your Assets, and Your Life*. 40.

6. Bok, 85. As Bok says, "Lying requires a *reason*, while truth-telling does not." 22. (Bok's emphasis)

7. *The Portable Machiavelli*. 75.

Chapter 9 – Forgiveness

T.S. Eliot. In his poem "Gerontion"

1. Robert D. Enright and Richard P. Fitzgibbons. *Helping Clients Forgive*. 24.

2. James K. McNulty. "Forgiveness Increases the Likelihood of Subsequent Partner Transgressions in Marriage."

3. James K. McNulty. "The Dark Side of Forgiveness: The Tendency to Forgive Predicts Continued Psychological and Physical Aggression in Marriage."

4. C.D. Frith. "Chapter 2 Perception." 21-23, fig. 2.9(c).

5. Nancy Berns. *Closure: The Rush to End Grief and What It Costs Us*. 22-23.

6. Ibid., 28.

Chapter 10 – Why Peggy Cried

Ayn Rand. "The Objectivist Ethics" in *The Virtue of Selfishness*. Slightly reworded. The exact wording is, "He is free to make the wrong choice, but not free to succeed with it."

1. Peggy Vaughan. *Preventing Affairs*. vii-viii.

2. James & Peggy Vaughan. *Beyond Affairs*.

3. If 80% of marriages involve affairs, as she claims, why is Peggy upset? Affairs are the norm (7). She objects to using the word "betrayal." (23). Yet in *Beyond Affairs* she admits James' deception was so crafty it called the whole pattern of her memory in question. She also claims affairs are society's fault. "…all of us are responsible for the factors in society that contribute to" affairs (10). "As a society, we need to acknowledge our role in perpetuating affairs…" (228). Peggy Vaughan. *The Monogamy Myth*.

4. Anne Bercht. *My Husband's Affair Became the Best Thing That Ever Happened to Me*.

5. R.J. Bulman and Camille Wortman. "Attributions of blame and coping in the "real world": severe accident victims react to their lot."

6. Bercht, 327.

7. Melvin J. Lerner. *The Belief in a Just World: A Fundamental Delusion*. 18.

8. Ibid., 31-36.

9. Ibid., 106.

10. Ibid., 40-53, 70-71.

11. Cynthia L. Pickett and Marilyn B. Brewer. "The Role of Exclusion in Maintaining Ingroup Inclusion." 89-111.

Also see Breakwell. 104-105, especially fig 4.3.

Chapter 11 – Adultery Apologists
William Ian Miller. *The Anatomy of Disgust*. 212.

1. Don-David Lusterman. *Infidelity: A Survival Guide*.

2. Ibid., 26.

3. Ibid., 8.

4. Ibid., 6.

5. Ibid., 65.

6. Robert Cialdini. *Influence: The Psychology of Persuasion*. 67-71.

7. Ibid., 73.

8. Janis Abrahms Spring. *After the Affair: Healing the Pain and Rebuilding Trust When a Partner Has Been Unfaithful*. 2nd Rev. ed., 2.

9. Mira Kirshenbaum, *When Good People Have Affairs: Inside the Hearts & Minds of Two People in Two Relationships*.

10. Spring, 2.

11. Ibid., 183. Compare to her "confront how you each contributed to the infidelity", 6. Compare to her statement to the unfaithful partner: "you have every right to address how your partner contributed to your dissatisfaction." 59.

12. Ibid., 85.

13. Esther Perel. *The State of Affairs Rethinking Infidelity*. xv.

14. Ibid., 45.

15. Ibid., 50.

16. Ibid., 43.

17. Ibid., 215.

18. Ibid., 214-217.

19. Ibid., 94.

20. Ibid., 292-296, 298-301.

21. Ibid., jealousy 94, courage 216, trust 299.

22. Zoe Heller. "In Defense of Adulterers." *The New Yorker*, Dec 18 & 25, 2017 Issue.

23. Pascal Boyer. *Religion Explained: The Evolutionary Origins of Religious Thought.* 186-187.

Chapter 12 - The Other Woman (or Man)
Ahmadou Kourouma. In James Geary, *Geary's Guide to the World's Great Aphorists*.

1. Melissa McTernan, Patrick Love, and David Rettinger. "The Influence of Personality on the Decision to Cheat."

Chapter 13 - Should I Tell?
Bo Bennett. In the TV series Criminal Minds, *Foundation* [7:18].

Chapter 14 - Cheating: Effects on Children
Robert Fulghum. In Bonita Zimmer. *Reflections for Tending the Sacred Garden: Embracing the Art of Slowing Down*, 182.

1. Lynn D. Wardle. "Parental Infidelity and the "No-Harm" Rule in Custody Litigation." 105.

2. Kate Figes. "How to ruin your child's chance of a happy love life: Have an affair—and the damage is WORSE the older they are when you stray." DailyMail.com, 22 Apr 2013.

3. Schiraldi, 41-42.

4. Wardle, 108.

Chapter 15 - Effects On You
Frans de Waal. *Good Natured*. 186.

1. Robert Cooter, "Hand Rule Damages for Incompensable Losses." 1097-1098.

2. Daniel Kahneman and Dale T. Miller. "Norm Theory: Comparing Reality to Its Alternatives." 353-354, 357.

3. Daniel T. Gilbert. "Inferential Correction." 169. Other aspects of stigma are discussed in Aphrodite Matsakis. *I Can't Get Over It: A Handbook for Trauma Survivors*. 91.

4. Paul Slovic. "Introduction and Overview." *The Perception of Risk*. xxvi. For stigma in technology, see: Robin Gregory, James Flynn, and Paul Slovic. "Technological Stigma."

As William Ian Miller remarks about those with a physical stigma, "we are never certain what we are supposed to do in their presence." *The Anatomy of Disgust*, 200.

5. A discussion of decision evasion is found in Philip E. Tetlock. "Intuitive Politicians, Theologians, and Prosecutors: Exploring the Empirical Implications of Deviant Functionalist Metaphors." 582-599.

6. Scott Plous. *The Psychology of Judgment and Decision Making*. 245-246.

7. de Waal (1996), 186.

Chapter 16 - What To Do Now
Kim Basinger. From IMDM.com. (retrieved 3 Dec 2018)

1. Cialdini, 105, 109.

2. Watkins. *Coherence*, 108.

3. Brian Tracy. *Time Power: A Proven System for Getting More Done in Less Time Than You Ever Thought Possible*, 268-269.

4. Gary Klein. "Performing a Project Premortem."

5. Gretchen B. Chapman and Eric J Johnson. "Incorporating the Irrelevant." 122.

6. Edward Teach. "Avoiding Decision Traps." CFO Magazine, 1 June 2004.

Chapter 17 - Accept
Warren Buffett. Mary Buffett and David Clark. *The Tao of Warren Buffett*. 38.

1. Ron Lieber. "American Express Kept a (Very) Watchful Eye on Charges." New York Times, 31 Jan 2009. The company was CompuCredit.

2. "Persons who are judged to share values which the individual believes are important to the making of decisions and the taking of actions in a particular domain (i.e., salient values) will be trusted." George Cvetkovich. "The Attribution of Social Trust." 55.

3. A more fully developed version of this is Identity Process Theory. See Breakwell, 261.

4. Ulrich Beck. "Living in the world risk society." 333.

Chapter 18 - Recover
Henry Kissinger. Often quoted, original source unknown.

1. Tina Seelig. *Creativity Rules: Get Ideas Out of Your Head and Into the World*. 56-58.

2. Bill Burnett and Dave Evans. *Designing Your Life: How to Build a Well-Lived, Joyful Life*.

3. Ayse Birsel. *Design the Life You Love: A Step-by-Step Guide to Building a Meaningful Future*.

4. Schiraldi, Appendix K, 417-418.

5. Spencer Eth, a psychiatrist, surveyed 225 people who escaped from the Twin Towers on 9/11. Experts had suggested psychoanalytically based therapy and cognitive behavioral therapy would be most helpful to survivors. Those surveyed, however, reported acupuncture, massage, yoga, and EMDR (eye movement desensitization and reprocessing) as most helpful. In Bessel van der Kolk. *The Body Keeps the Score: Brain, Mind, and Body in the Healing of Trauma*. 230-231.

6. Jenny Blake. *Pivot: The Only Move That Matters Is Your Next One.* 110-111.

7. A starting point is: James Joseph. *Every Man's Guide to Ballroom Dancing,* 123, or James Joseph. *Hear the Beat, Feel the Music.*

8. David Allen. *Getting Things Done: The Art of Stress-Free Productivity.* 34-35.

9. William Samuelson and Richard Zeckhauser. "Status Quo Bias in Decision Making."

Chapter 19 - Disconnect
R. Scott Bakker. *The Darkness That Comes Before.* New York: Overlook, 2008.

1. Jasmine Lee Cori. *Healing from Trauma: A Survivor's Guide to Understanding Your Symptoms and Reclaiming Your Life.* 3-4.

2. For example, Shirley Glass. *Not "Just Friends": Protect Your Relationship from Infidelity and Heal the Trauma of Betrayal.* New York: Free Press, 2003. (The book now carries the subtitle *Rebuilding Trust and Recovering Your Sanity After Infidelity.* Whatever the subtitle, it appears to be the identical book.)

Shirley Glass suggests looking at your relationship in terms of 'walls' and 'windows'. That's how one deals with a recalcitrant teenager, not a genuine life partner. 12-13, 25-26.

When Glass claims there is a "new infidelity" in which affairs don't have to be sexual, it becomes impossible to tell what the 210 "unfaithful" people in her study did. There is no breakdown by year, gender, and specific behavior. She reports results in percentages, not numbers, making it even more difficult to analyze her claims. 1-2.

Glass introduces side issues to obscure the main issue. For example, when she discusses the lies of cheaters, she claims the real question is whether the cheater lied because they cheated or lied because they are a chronic liar. That's like asking, did the murderer lie to the police because of the murder or because he habitually lies. The answer makes no difference. 60.

Chapter 20 - Conclusion
Orson Welles. Apparently the quote is from Welles' screenplay for *The Big Brass Ring.*

1. Thomas More. *Utopia.* Book 2, 84-85.

WORKS CITED

Abrams, Dominic, Michael A. Hogg, and Jose M. Marques (eds.). *The Social Psychology of Inclusion and Exclusion.* New York: Psychology Press, 2005.

Alhakami, Ali Siddiq and Paul Slovic. "A Psychological Study of the Inverse Relationship Between Perceived Risk and Perceived Benefit." *Risk Analysis* 1994, 14 (6): 1085-1096.

Allen, David. *Getting Things Done: The Art of Stress-Free Productivity.* New York: Penguin, 2001.

Aristotle. *Nicomachean Ethics.* Translated by W.D. Ross. Oxford: Clarendon Press, 1908. classics.mit.edu/Aristotle/nicomachaen.mb.txt (retrieved 7 July 2019)

Armor, David A. and Shelley E. Taylor. "When Predictions Fail: The Dilemma of Unrealistic Optimism." (2002) In Gilovich.

Arnett, Jeffrey Jensen and Joseph Schwab. "The Clark University Poll of Emerging Adults." Dec 2012. PDF.

Baker, Lynn A. and Robert E. Emery. "When Every Relationship Is Above Average." *Law and Human Behavior* 1993, 17 (4): 439-450.

Beck, Ulrich. "Living in the world risk society." *Economy and Society* 2006, 35 (3): 329-345.

Bercht, Anne. *My Husband's Affair Became the Best Thing That Ever Happened to Me.* Victoria BC: Trafford, 2004.

Berkes, Howard. "Hero Pilot in 1989 United Crash Dies." NPR 10 May 2012. https://www.npr.org/blogs/thetwo-way/2012/05/10/152402632/hero-pilot-in-1989-united-crash-dies (NPR deleted the Two-Way in 2018.)

Berns, Nancy. *Closure: The Rush to End Grief and What It Can Cost Us.* Philadelphia: Temple University Press, 2011.

Betzig, Laura. "Causes of Conjugal Dissolution: A Cross-cultural Study." *Current Anthropology* 1989, 30 (5): 654-76.

Birsel, Ayse. *Design the Life You Love: A Step-by-Step Guide to Building a Meaningful Future.* New York: Ten Speed Press, 2015.

Blake, Jenny. *Pivot: The Only Move That Matters Is Your Next One.* New York: Portfolio/Penguin, 2016.

Bok, Sissela. *Lying: Moral Choice in Public and Private Life.* New York: Vintage, 1999.

Boyer, Pascal. *Religion Explained: The Evolutionary Origins of Religious Thought.* New York: Basic Books, 2001.

Breakwell, Glynis M. *The Psychology of Risk.* New York: Cambridge University Press, 2007.

Brosnan, Sarah F. and Frans B. M. de Waal. "Monkeys Reject Unequal Pay." *Nature* 18 Sep 2003, 425: 297-299.

Buffett, Mary and David Clark. *The Tao of Warren Buffett.* New York: Scribner, 2006.

Bulman, R.J., and Camille Wortman. "Attributions of blame and coping in the "real world": severe accident victims react to their lot." *Journal of Personality and Social Psychology* 1977, 35 (5): 351-63.

Burnett, Bill and Dave Evans. *Designing Your Life: How to Build a Well-Lived, Joyful Life.* New York: Knopf, 2016.

Caldwell, Benjamin. "Is it couple therapy, couple's therapy, or couples therapy?" Psychotherapy Notes, 2 July 2018, www.psychotherapynotes.com/couple-therapy-couples-therapy/ (retrieved 12 June 2019)

Cameron, Julia. *The Artist's Way.* New York: TarcherPerigee, Anniversary Ed., 2016.

206

Carli, Linda L. "Cognitive Reconstruction, Hindsight, and Reactions to Victims and Perpetrators." *Personality and Social Psychology Bulletin* 1999, 25 (8): 966-979.

Carnahan, Ann. "Beyond Survival: Life's trials continued for pilot after 1989 crash (Al Haynes United Flight 232)." Rocky Mountain News, 7 May 2005.

Chapman, Gretchen B. and Eric J Johnson. "Incorporating the Irrelevant." (2002) In Gilovich.

Charny, Israel and S. Parnass. "The Impact of Extramarital Relationships on the Continuation of Marriages." *Journal of Sex & Marital Therapy* 1995, 21 (2): 100-115.

Cialdini, Robert. *Influence: The Psychology of Persuasion.* New York: Harper Business, 2006.

Conway, Michael and Michael Ross. "Getting what you want by revising what you had." *Journal of Personality and Social Psychology* 1984, 47 (4): 738-748.

Cooter, Robert. "Hand Rule Damages for Incompensable Losses." 40 San Diego L. Rev. 1097 (2003).

Cori, Jasmine Lee. *Healing from Trauma: A Survivor's Guide to Understanding Your Symptoms and Reclaiming Your Life.* New York: Da Capo, 2008.

Cosmides, Leda and John Tooby. "Evolutionary Psychology: A Primer." Center for Evolutionary Psychology, University of California, Santa Barbara website. (1997). cep.ucsb.edu/primer.html (retrieved 07 July 2019)

Cosmides, Leda and John Tooby. "Social Exchange: The Evolutionary Design of a Neurocognitive System." In Michael S. Gazzaniga, (ed.), *The New Cognitive Neurosciences III.* Cambridge MA: MIT Press, 2005.

Cosmides, Leda, H. Clark Garrett, and John Tooby. "Adaptive Specializations, Social Exchange, and the Evolution of Human Intelligence." PNAS (Proceedings of the National Academy of Sciences) 11 May 2010, 107 (Supplement 2) 9007-9014.

Cvetkovich, George. "The Attribution of Social Trust." In George Cvetkovich and Ragnar E. Lofstedt (eds.), *Social Trust and the Management of Risk.* London: Earthscan, 2013.

Damasio, Antonio R. *Descartes' Error: Emotion, Reason, and the Human Brain*. New York: Putnam, 1994.

de Waal, Frans. *Good Natured: the origins of right and wrong in humans and other animals*. Cambridge MA: Harvard University Press, 1996.

de Waal, Frans. *Our Inner Ape*. New York: Riverhead Books, 2005.

du Maurier, Daphne. *The House on the Strand*. Philadelphia: University of Pennsylvania Press, 2000.

Dunning, David, Judith A. Meyerowitz, and Amy D. Holzberg. "Ambiguity and Self-Evaluation: The Role of Idiosyncratic Trait Definitions in Self-Serving Assessments of Ability." (1978, 2002) In Gilovich.

Edwards, Elizabeth. *Resilience: Reflections on the Burdens and Gifts of Facing Life's Adversities*. (New Afterward Edition) New York: Broadway Books, 2010.

Ekman, Paul. *Emotions Revealed: Recognizing Faces and Feelings to Improve Communication and Emotional Life*. 2nd ed. New York: Holt Paperbacks, 2007.

Enright, Robert D. and Richard P. Fitzgibbons. *Helping Clients Forgive*. Washington DC: American Psychological Association, 2000.

Figes, Kate. "How to ruin your child's chance of a happy love life: Have an affair—and the damage is WORSE the older they are when you stray." DailyMail.com, 22 Apr 2013. (retrieved 13 July 2019)

Foreman, Judy. "A Conversation With: Paul Ekman." New York Times, 5 Aug 2003.

Frith. C. D. "Chapter 2 Perception." In H. J. Eysenck and G. D. Wilson (eds.), *A Textbook of Human Psychology*. Lancaster, England: MTP, 1976.

Gates, Dominic. "20 Years Ago, Pilot's Heroic Efforts Saved 185 People As Plane Crashed." *Seattle Times*, 19 Jul 2009.

Gershman, Jacob. "Crash Diary No. 2." *New York Magazine*, 1 Feb 2009.

Gilbert, Daniel T. "Inferential Correction." (2002) In Gilovich.

Gilovich, Thomas, Dale Griffin, and Daniel Kahneman (eds.). *Heuristics and Biases: The Psychology of Intuitive Judgment*. New York: Cambridge University Press, 2002.

Glass, Shirley. *Not "Just Friends": Protect Your Relationship from Infidelity and Heal the Trauma of Betrayal*. New York: Free Press, 2003. This book has also been published with the subtitle *Rebuilding Trust and Recovering Your Sanity After Infidelity*.

Godfrey, Joe. "Al Haynes." AVweb 29 Sep 1999. avweb.com/features/al-haynes/ (retrieved 08 July 2019)

Gray, Mark M., Paul M. Perl, and Tricia C. Bruce. "Marriage in the Catholic Church." Center for Applied Research in the Apostolate, Washington DC: Georgetown University, Oct 2007. PDF

Gregory, Robin, James Flynn, and Paul Slovic. "Technological Stigma." *American Scientist* 1995, 83 (3), 220-223.

Hadaway, C. Kirk and Penny Long Marler. "How Many Americans Attend Worship Each Week? An Alternative Approach to Measurement." *Journal for the Scientific Study of Religion* 2005, 44 (3): 307-322.

Haidt, Jonathan. "The Emotional Dog and its Rational Tail: A Social Intuitionist Approach to Moral Judgment." *Psychological Review* 2001, 108 (4): 814-834.

Harris, Chrys J. "Sensory-based Therapy for Crisis Counselors." In Figley, Charles R. (ed.), *Compassion Fatigue: coping with secondary traumatic stress disorder in those who treat the traumatized*. New York: Routledge, 1995.

Haynes, Al. "The Crash of United Flight 232 by Capt. Al Haynes." Recorded speech. NASA-Dryden, 24 May 1991.

Heller, Zoe. "In Defense of Adulterers." *The New Yorker*, Dec 18 & 25, 2017 Issue. (retrieved 10 June 2019)

Herman, Judith. "Chapter 8 Safety." *Trauma and Recovery*. New York: Basic Books, 1992.

International Society for Traumatic Stress Studies. "Clinician Administered PTSD Scale (CAPS)" (n.d.). www.istss.org/assessing-trauma/clinician-administered-ptsd-scale-(caps). aspx (retrieved 11 June 2019)

Joseph, James. *Every Man's Guide to Ballroom Dancing.* Jackson Hole WY: BlueChip Publishers, 2014.

Joseph, James. *Hear the Beat, Feel the Music.* Jackson Hole WY: BlueChip Publishers, 2018.

Kahneman, Daniel and Dale T. Miller. "Norm Theory: Comparing Reality to Its Alternatives." (1986, 2002) In Gilovich.

Kahneman, Daniel and Shane Frederick. "Representativeness Revisited: Attribute Substitution in Intuitive Judgment." (2002) In Gilovich.

Kahneman, Daniel, Paul Slovic, and Amos Tversky (eds.). *Judgment under uncertainty: Heuristics and biases.* Cambridge, England: Cambridge University Press, 1982.

Kirshenbaum, Mira. *When Good People Have Affairs: Inside the Hearts & Minds of Two People in Two Relationships.* New York: St. Martin's, 2008.

Klein, Gary. "Performing a Project Premortem." *Harvard Business Review* 2007, 85 (9): 18-19.

Knopp, Kayla, Shelby B. Scott, Lane Ritchie, Galena K. Rhoades, Howard J. Markman, and Scott M. Stanley. "Once a Cheater, Always a Cheater? Serial Infidelity Across Subsequent Relationships." *Archives of Sexual Behavior* 2017, 46 (8): 2301-2311.

Lerner, Melvin J. *The Belief in a Just World: A Fundamental Delusion.* New York: Plenum, 1980.

Lewis, C.S. *Till We Have Faces: A Myth Retold.* New York: Harper One, reissue ed., 2017.

Lewis, Neil A. "For Edwards, Drama Builds Toward a Denouement." New York Times, 20 Sep 2009.

Lieber, Ron. "American Express Kept a (Very) Watchful Eye on Charges." New York Times, 31 Jan 2009.

Luna, J. J. *How to Be Invisible: Protect Your Home, Your Children, Your Assets, and Your Life*. New York: Thomas Dunne Books, rev. ed., 2004.

Lusterman, Don-David. *Infidelity: A Survival Guide*. Oakland CA: New Harbinger, 1998.

Machiavelli, Niccolò. *The Portable Machiavelli*. Peter Bondanella and Mark Musa (trans.). New York: Penguin 1979.

Magnussen, Svein and Annika Melinder. "What Psychologists Know and Believe about Memory: A Survey of Practitioners." *Applied Cognitive Psychology* 2012, 26 (1): 54-60.

Manitoba Trauma Information & Education Centre. "Phases of Trauma Recovery." Unsigned article. 2013. trauma-recovery.ca/recovery/phases-of-trauma-recovery/ (retrieved 11 June 2019)

Matsakis, Aphrodite. *I Can't Get Over It: A Handbook for Trauma Survivors*. Oakland CA: New Harbinger, 2nd rev. ed, 1996.

McNulty, James K. "Forgiveness Increases the Likelihood of Subsequent Partner Transgressions in Marriage." *Journal of Family Psychology* 2010, 24 (6): 787-790.

McNulty, James K. "The Dark Side of Forgiveness: The Tendency to Forgive Predicts Continued Psychological and Physical Aggression in Marriage." *Personality and Social Psychology Bulletin* 2011, 37 (6): 770-783.

McTernan, Melissa, Patrick Love, and David Rettinger. "The Influence of Personality on the Decision to Cheat." *Ethics and Behavior* 2014, 24 (1): 53-72.

Miller, William Ian. *The Anatomy of Disgust*. Cambridge MA: Harvard University Press, 1997.

More, Thomas. *Utopia*. George M Logan (ed.) and Robert M. Adams, (trans.), 3rd ed.. New York: Cambridge University Press, 2016.

Panskepp, Jaak. *Affective Neuroscience: The Foundations of Human and Animal Emotion.* New York: Oxford University Press, 1998.

Perel, Esther. *The State of Affairs: Rethinking Infidelity.* New York: HarperCollins, 2017.

Pickett, Cynthia L. and Marilyn B. Brewer. "The Role of Exclusion in Maintaining In-group Inclusion." In Dominic Abrams, Michael A. Hogg, and Jose M. Marques (eds.), *The Social Psychology of Inclusion and Exclusion.* New York: Psychology Press, 2005.

Plous, Scott. *The Psychology of Judgment and Decision Making.* New York: McGraw-Hill, 1993.

Plutchik, Robert. "A General Psychoevolutionary Theory of Emotion." In Robert Plutchik and Henry Kellerman (eds.), *Emotion Theory, Research, and Experience,* Vol. 1. New York: Academic Press, 1980.

Porter, Stephen and Kristine A. Peace. "The Scars of Memory: A prospective, longitudinal investigation of the consistency of traumatic and positive emotional memories in adulthood." *Psychological Science* 2007, 18 (5): 435-441.

Prinz, Jesse J. *Gut Reactions: A Perceptual Theory of Emotion.* New York: Oxford University Press, 2004.

Rothbart, Myron and Bernadette Park. "On the Confirmability and Disconfirmability of Trait Concepts." *Journal of Personality and Social Psychology* 1986, 50 (1): 131-142.

Rothschild, Babette. *8 Keys to Safe Trauma Recovery: Take-Charge Strategies to Empower Your Healing.* New York: W. W. Norton, 2010.

Rozin, Paul and April Fallon. "The Acquisition of Likes and Dislikes for Foods." In *What Is America Eating?* Washington DC: National Academy Press, 1986.

Rozin, Paul, Jonathan Haidt, and Clark R. McCauley. "Disgust." In Michael Lewis, Jeannette M. Haviland-Jones, and Lisa Feldman Barrett (eds.), *Handbook of Emotions,* 3rd ed. New York: Guilford Press, 2008.

Samuelson, William and Richard Zeckhauser. "Status Quo Bias in Decision Making." *Journal of Risk and Uncertainty* 1988, 1 (1): 7-59.

Schank, Roger C. *Tell Me a Story: Narrative and Intelligence (Rethinking Theory)*. Evanston IL: Northwestern University Press, 1995.

Schiraldi, Glenn R. *The Post-Traumatic Stress Disorder Sourcebook: A Guide to Healing, Recovery, and Growth*, 2nd ed. New York: McGraw-Hill Education, 2016.

Seelig, Tina. *Creativity Rules: Get Ideas Out of Your Head and Into the World*. New York: HarperCollins, 2017.

Slovic, Paul. "Introduction and Overview." In Paul Slovic (ed.), *The Perception of Risk*. London: Earthscan, 2000.

Slovic, Paul. "Perceived Risk, Trust and Democracy." In Paul Slovic (ed.), *The Perception of Risk*. London: Earthscan, 2000.

Spring, Janis Abrahms. *After the Affair: Healing the Pain and Rebuilding Trust When a Partner Has Been Unfaithful*. New York: Harper, 2nd Rev. ed., 2012.

Stephens-Davidowitz, Seth. *Everybody Lies: Big Data, New Data, and What the Internet Can Tell Us About Who We Really Are*. New York: Dey Street, 2018.

Swiss Center for Affective Sciences. "The Grid Project." (n.d.) https://www.affective-sciences.org/research/topics/specific-research-projects/language-and-culture/grid-project/ (retrieved 10 June 2019)

Tabibnia, Golnaz, Ajay B. Satpute, and Matthew D. Lieberman. "The Sunny Side of Fairness: Preference for fairness activates reward circuitry (and disregarding unfairness activates self-control circuitry)." *Psychological Science* 2008, 19 (4): 339-347.

Taleb, Nassim Nicholas. *The Black Swan: The Impact of the Highly Improbable*. New York: Random House, 2007.

Teach, Edward. "Avoiding Decision Traps." CFO Magazine, 1 June 2004.

Tetlock, Philip E. "Intuitive Politicians, Theologians, and Prosecutors: Exploring the Empirical Implications of Deviant Functionalist Metaphors." (2002) In Gilovich.

213

Tracy, Brian. *Time Power: A Proven System for Getting More Done in Less Time Than You Ever Thought Possible.* New York: AMACOM, 2007.

Tversky, Amos and Daniel Kahneman. "Extensional versus Intuitive Reasoning: The Conjunction Fallacy in Probability Judgment." (1984) In Gilovich.

Tversky, Amos and Daniel Kahneman. "Judgments of and by Representativeness." In Daniel Kahneman, Paul Slovic, and Amos Tversky (eds.), *Judgment under uncertainty: Heuristics and biases.* Cambridge England: Cambridge University Press, 1982.

Tversky, Amos and Derek J. Koehler. "Support Theory: A Nonextensional Representation of Subjective Probability." *Psychological Review* 1994, 101 (4): 547-567.

Twitchell, James. "Chapter 8 - De Beers: A Good Campaign Is Forever." *Twenty Ads That Shook the World.* New York: Three Rivers, 2000.

U.S. Department of Veterans Affairs. "Clinician-Administered PTSD Scale for DSM-5 (CAPS-5)." www.ptsd.va.gov/professional/assessment/adult-int/caps.asp. (retrieved 11 June 2019.)

van der Kolk, Bessel. *The Body Keeps the Score: Brain, Mind, and Body in the Healing of Trauma.* New York: Penguin, 2014.

Vaughan, James & Peggy. *Beyond Affairs.* Hilton Head Island SC: Dialog Press, 1980.

Vaughan, Peggy. *The Monogamy Myth.* New York: Newmarket, 2003.

Vaughan, Peggy. *Preventing Affairs.* San Diego CA: Dialog Press, 2008.

Viroli, Maurizio. *Niccolo's Smile: A Biography of Machiavelli.* New York: Hill and Wang, 2000.

Walton, Jessica L., Lisa-Ann J. Cuccurullo, Amanda M. Raines, Desirae N. Vidaurri, Nicholas P. Allan. "Sometimes Less is More: Establishing the core symptoms of PTSD." *Journal of Traumatic Stress* 2017, 30 (3): 254-258.

Wardle, Lynn D. "Parental Infidelity and the "No-Harm" Rule in Custody Litigation," 52 Cath. U. L. Rev. 81 (2003).

Watkins, Alan. *Coherence: The Secret Science of Brilliant Leadership.* London: Kogan Page, 2014.

Watson, David. *Mood and Temperament.* New York: Guilford Press, 2000.

Whitehead, Barbara Dafoe and David Popenoe. "Singles Seek Soul Mates for Marriage." Gallup News Service, 27 June 2001.

Whitehead, Barbara Dafoe and David Popenoe. "Who Wants to Marry a Soul Mate?" *The State of Our Unions 2001.* New Brunswick NJ: Rutgers University, 2001.

Wilson, Timothy D., David B. Centerbar, and Nancy Brekke. "Mental Contamination and the Debiasing Problem." (2002) In Gilovich.

Woodruff, Bob (interviewer). "Transcript: John Edwards Interview: Read selections of Bob Woodruff's Interview With John Edwards." *ABC Nightline,* 8 Aug 2008.

Zak, Dan. "The Truth About Lying." Washington Post, 25 Nov 2007.

Zimering, Rose and Suzy Bird Gulliver. "Secondary Traumatization in Mental Health Care Providers." *Psychiatric Times* 2003, 20 (4).

Zimmer, Bonita. *Reflections for Tending the Sacred Garden: Embracing the Art of Slowing Down.* Lincoln NE: iUniverse, 2003.

Made in the USA
Monee, IL
11 December 2024

73284179R00125